# A STRATEGIC ATLAS

*The policy of a state lies in its geography.*
     —NAPOLEON

# A STRATEGIC ATLAS

## Comparative Geopolitics of the World's Powers

SECOND EDITION, REVISED AND UPDATED

# Gérard Chaliand and Jean-Pierre Rageau

*Translated from the French by Tony Berrett*

*Maps by Catherine Petit*

**HARPER & ROW, PUBLISHERS, New York**
Cambridge, Philadelphia, San Francisco, London
Mexico City, São Paulo, Sydney

THIS ATLAS IS DEDICATED

- to the British geopolitical analyst Halford J. Mackinder (1861–1947);

- to the theorist of sea power, the American Alfred T. Mahan (1840–1914);

- to the pioneer of geopolitics, the German Friedrich Ratzel (1844–1904);

- and to the French geographer Pierre Vidal de la Blache (1845–1918)

This work was originally published in France under the title *Atlas Stratégique,* © Librairie Arthème Fayard, 1983.

FIRST EDITION

ISBN: 0-06-015387-3

ISBN: 0-06-091220-0 (pbk.)

LIBRARY OF CONGRESS CATALOG CARD NUMBER: 84-48143

85 86 87 88 10 9 8 7 6 5 4 3 2 1

# PREFACE

This atlas is an innovation. No strategic atlas exists in English, French, or German—nor, so far as we are aware, in any other language. For this is not a mapping of past or future battles, or a graphic depiction of opposing military forces. Strategy, like politics, embraces war, but is more than war. What is provided here is truly a geopolitics of the relations of force in the contemporary world. In order to portray as accurately as possible realities that are at once multifaceted, complex, and sometimes impossible to represent at all (how, for example, to measure determination, which is of course a key factor in conflict situations? Can one predict surprise?), we have sought to be as global as possible.

From the outset, our perspective on our planet breaks with the Mercator projection, with its horizontal and almost pre-Galilean world, in which the land masses appear to cover a larger area than the seas. The modern perspective should give a more faithful picture of a globe on which the poles, the axes of the world, are, at least at the present time in the case of the Arctic, a decisive area that does not appear on the usual maps. We have therefore favored a multiplicity of projections, and these have been selected solely for the purposes of our demonstration, and to show every aspect of the world.

Thus, geographically our atlas gives considerable space to the oceans, which cover the larger part of the planet, on which sea power is engaged, mastery of which has ensured Anglo-American hegemony for almost two centuries: the Arctic Ocean whose frozen surfaces do not prevent the passage of nuclear submarines underneath; the Pacific, whose strong points are all controlled by the Anglo-Americans and the French; the Atlantic, both North and South; and the Indian Ocean, currently a delicate area where more than anywhere else today's rivalries manifest themselves.

We have also sought to show, in addition to the usual views and projections used by Europeans and Americans, the world as it is seen by the Chinese, the Soviets, and the Arab Muslims. We have sought to show the great cultural and religious domains, which are the matrices of world views, and in this way to complement our strategic approach with the historical background that shapes collective behaviors and that may determine external decisions to fight, or provoke imbalances within a society.

No attempt has ever been made, for example, to compile a map of the major traditional enmities that have determinied conflicts in a given historical epoch. How, for example, can we understand Poland without alluding to its dual rejection of the Russians and the Germans? However, our atlas is essentially centered on the at least militarily bipolarized world that emerged from World War II. It shows the present world strategic situation while at the same time indicating the changes that have occurred since the beginnings of the Cold War, both in the area of crises and in conventional conflicts or guerrilla activities.

This strategic atlas also looks at a dimension that is not treated in the usual works: states' perceptions of their security—not only those of the world powers (the United States or the Soviet Union), but also those of the lesser known regional powers such as Saudi Arabia, India, South Africa, Brazil, Japan, and Israel. It is, for example, not sufficiently appreciated that the security perceptions of a state such as Saudi Arabia are a function of its hostility not only to the Soviet Union and Israel, but also to the Soviet presence in Afghanistan, Ethiopia (an obstacle to Arab control of the Red Sea), and the Democratic Republic of Yemen on its southern flank; of its rejection of a regional hegemony by Shiite Iran; and finally of its own military and demographic weakness, half its working population being foreigners.

We have also tried to present a multiform world with very different perceptions*. Of course, our work includes a number of more conventional maps concerning agricultural, industrial, mineral, and energy resources, as well as demographic data and information making it possible to grasp the nature of North–South relations. Wherever it seemed useful, we have provided statistical projections up to the end of the century. Finally, our atlas includes a strictly military section, partly centered on nuclear questions. In short, our conception of strategy attempts to embrace the totality of human, material, and cultural factors that make up a global balance of forces.

As such, our atlas does not claim to be free of all shortcomings. But we are nevertheless certain that we are taking a novel approach to revealing the political realities of the contemporary world.

We would like to thank General Pierre Gallois, who looked at our military maps and generously provided two that he had drawn himself; Catherine Petit, our cartographer, for her work; and Claude Durand, who was from the beginning convinced of the novelty of our project and took on the risks involved.

Gérard Chaliand
Jean-Pierre Rageau

---

*Perhaps we have been helped in this by the fact that we both studied at the Ecole Nationale des Langues Orientales, one of the very few institutions where it was possible in the 1950s to acquire a view of the world that was not Western-centered.

# CONTENTS

# Polar Projection

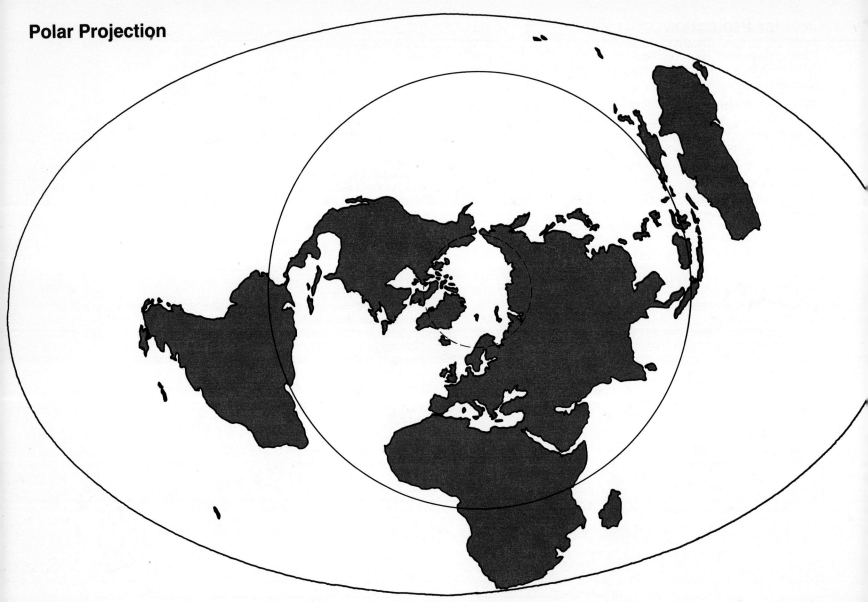

# Circular Projection

The earth is a sphere. Any representation of it on a two-dimensional plane is obtained by a projection. For example, the map on the left is a polar projection. For convenience, most maps and atlases use plane projections, which ignore the spherical nature of the globe. But this convention falsifies strategic perception as soon as it goes beyond the regional level. The circular projection on the right is modified, and hence misleading, but serves to illustrate our point.

11

# A Militarily Bipolar World

China, which is militarily hostile to the USSR, cannot be included among the West's allies. (For the African states linked to France by assistance agreements, see the section on Africa.)

USA
U.S. allies
China
USSR allies

cartography: Catherine Petit

# VIEWS OF THE WORLD

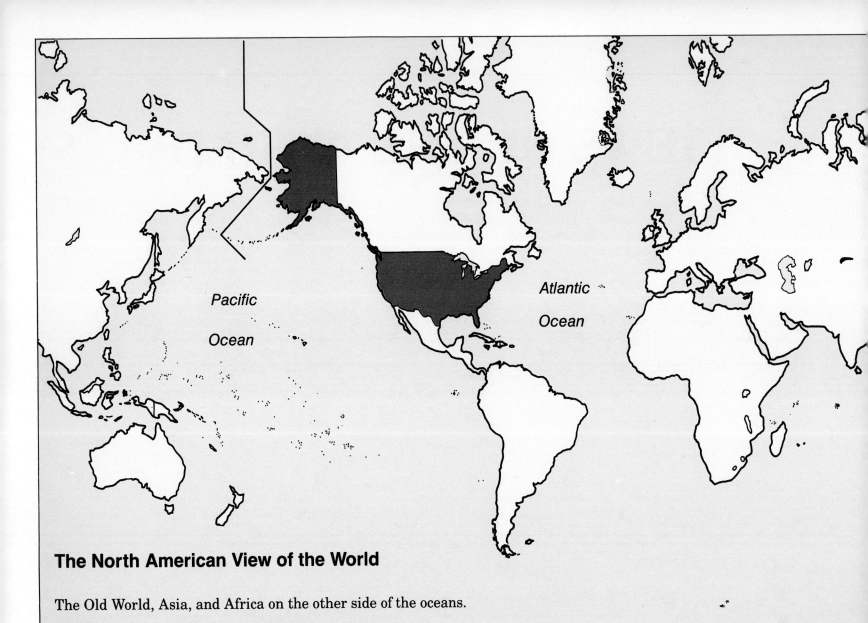

Pacific

Ocean

Atlantic

Ocean

# The North American View of the World

The Old World, Asia, and Africa on the other side of the oceans.

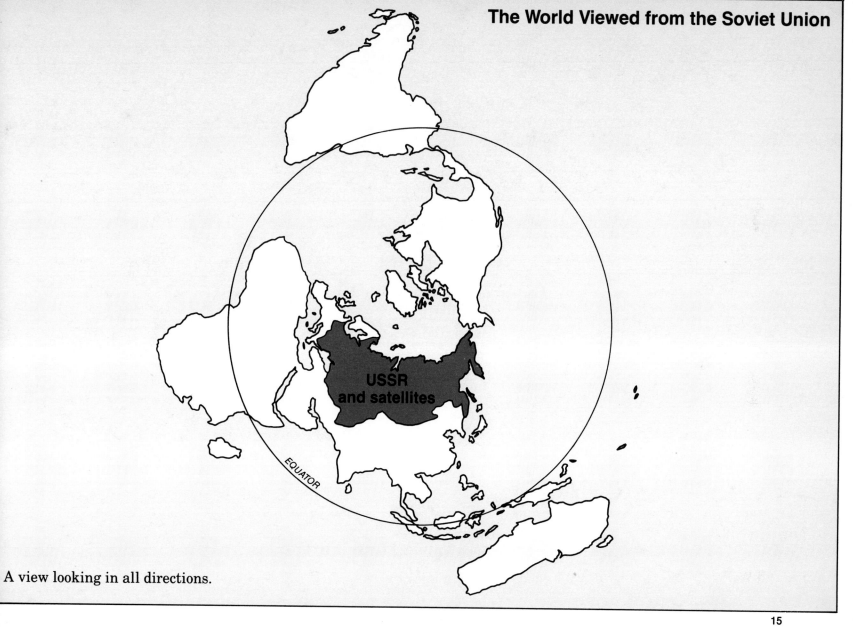

USSR
and satellites

EQUATOR

A view looking in all directions.

## The World Viewed from Europe

A familiar view.

Arctic Ocean

EUROPE

ASIA

Bering Strait

Bay of Alaska

AMERICA

AFRICA

Atlantic Ocean

Yellow Sea

East China Sea

Arabian Sea

Bay of Bengal

South China Sea

Pacific Ocean
(Ocean of Great Peace)

Atlantic Ocean

AMERICA

Indian Ocean

Coral Sea

AUSTRALIA
(Continent of the Great Ocean)

Tasman Sea

ANTARCTICA

## The World Viewed from China

From the *Contemporary Atlas of the People's Republic of China.*

# Arab Muslim View of the World

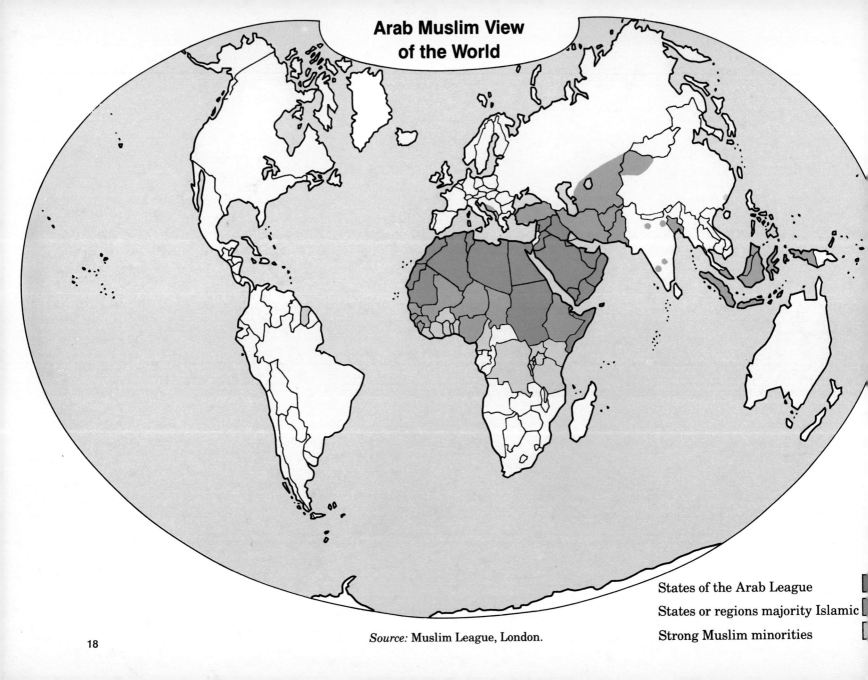

States of the Arab League

States or regions majority Islamic

Strong Muslim minorities

*Source:* Muslim League, London.

# THE GEOPOLITICIANS

# The Geopoliticians

The German geographer Friedrich Ratzel, author of *Politische Geographie* (1897), developed a number of basic concepts, particularly concerning *space,* that have inspired geopoliticians. It was the British writer H. Mackinder who in 1904 proposed the notion that the continental part of Eurasia, by virtue of its land mass, forms the world Heartland. According to Mackinder (maps pp. 21 and 22), who several times revised his geographical delimitation of the heartland (in 1919 and 1943), the power that controls this land mass—once potentially Germany, now the Soviet Union—threatens the sea powers—once Great Britain, now the United States—that control the World Island—that is, our planet.

The factors that Mackinder came to include as his thinking developed were communications (including aviation), population, and industrialization. In 1943, he repudiated his 1919 theory (the state that controls the Heartland will dominate the World Island).

The American Mahan, a geopolitician before the word was invented, put forward as early as 1900 (in *The Problem of Asia and Its Effect upon International Politics*) the idea that the world hegemony of sea powers can be maintained by control of a series of bases around the Eurasian continent. This view foreshadowed Mackinder's concept of the World Island, but it led to the opposite strategic conclusions: Sea powers dominate land powers by hemming them in. Therein lies the seed of the theory of containment born of the Cold War.

Geopolitical conceptions were systematized by the Swede Rudolf Kjellen and then adopted by the German geopoliticians, especially Karl Haushofer (1869–1946). German geopolitics developed in three directions: the concept of space *(Raum)* brought out by Ratzel, meaning the need for a great power to have space available to it; the concept of a World Island enunciated by Mackinder, implying sea power; and the North–South combination of continents put forward by Haushofer (map p. 24). This latter conception is to be found today, for example, in the Eurafrican policy of Western Europe.

The American N. J. Spykman (map p. 23) followed Mackinder and adapted his concepts to the circumstances of the 1930s. He argued that only an Anglo-American (sea power) and Russian (land power) alliance could prevent Germany from controlling the Eurasian coastal regions and thus achieving world domination. But he rejected some of Mackinder's strategic conclusions concerning the importance of controlling the Heartland by giving greater importance to control of the Rimland.

Although it is sometimes excessively systematic, the geopolitical approach is stimulating; but it is so only if there is no lapse into geographical determinism and if all factors in the balance are taken into account. In the map on p. 25 we sketch our own approach along these lines, one more in conformity with present-day realities.

# The World according to Mackinder (1904)

Control of the Heartland, the Eurasian continental land mass, constitutes a potential threat for sea powers.

EXTERIOR

HEARTLAND
(Central Zone)

EXTERIOR

RING

OF

ISLANDS

INTERIOR

OR

MARGINAL

RING

OR

OUTER

CONTINENTS

# The World according to Mackinder (1943)

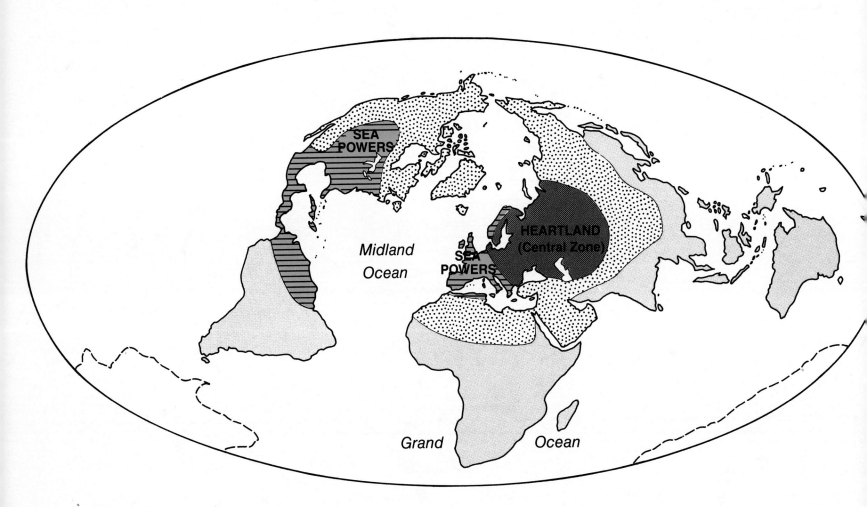

SEA POWERS

SEA POWERS

HEARTLAND (Central Zone)

Midland

Ocean

Grand        Ocean

# Spykman and the Importance of the Rimland

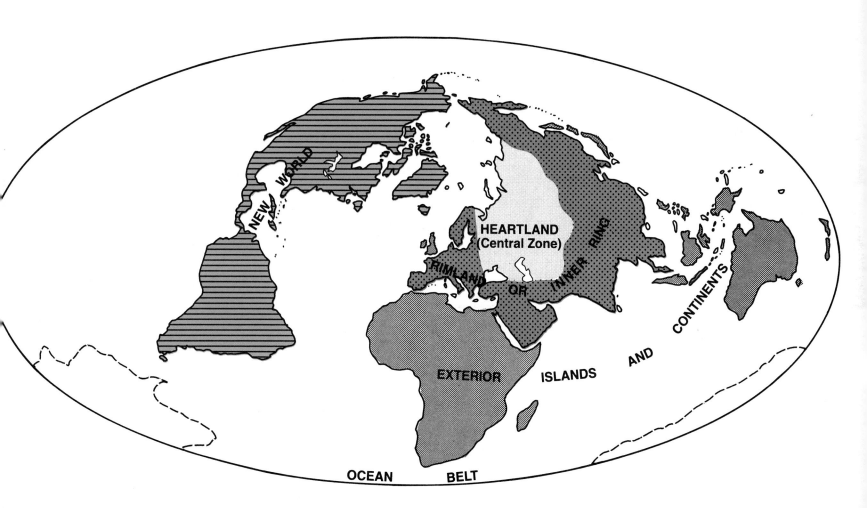

# Haushofer and the North–South Combination

PAN-

EURAFRICA

PAN-RUSSIA

Berlin

EAST ASIAN
CO-PROSPERITY
SPHERE

Tokyo

EURAFRICA

AMERICA

# Sketch of a Contemporary Geopolitics

Taking into account inevitable developments and changes, we see that geopoliticians before World War II accurately assessed these basic factors:
- *Heartland*
- *Sea power*
- *Rimland*

We also see the appearance since 1945, with the independence of new states in Asia and Africa, of a fragile and unstable intertropical ring:
- *Ring of underdevelopment and poverty*

Gradual emergence of a *developed southern ring* is linked to sea power.

# CULTURAL FACTORS

# The Great Cultural Domains

The cultural area of which Europe is the center has undergone considerable expansion. So has that of Islam which, in Southeast Asia, covers regions that were formerly Hindu, while at the same time continuing its expansion in Africa.*

*Madagascar is attached to Africa for the sake of convenience, but ethnically does not belong to the African world.

European domain

Chinese domain

Russo-Soviet domain

Islamic domain

Black African domain

Hindu domain

Latin American domain

South Africa (mixed)

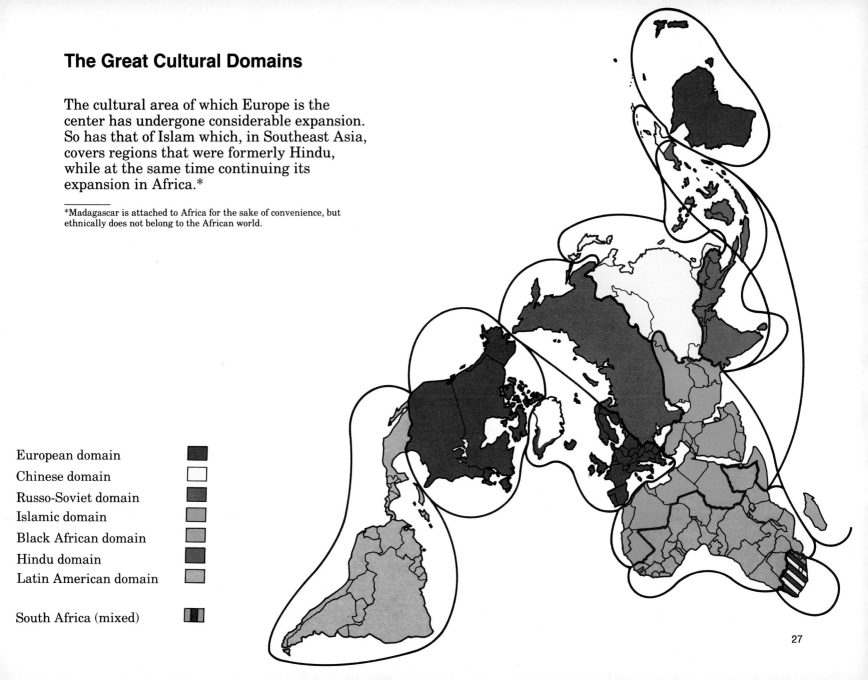

# The Great Religions

Religions were formerly the major source of
identity, and since nationalism, rather than
superseding religion, is often superimposed on
it, religions continue to play a leading role.

*Notes:*
- Oriental Christians: principally Orthodox
- China: superimposition and
  interdependence of Confucianism,
  Buddhism, Taoism
- Japan: superimposition of Shintoism and
  Buddhism
- Gray areas: animism and others

Catholicism

Protestantism

Oriental Christians

Islam (Sunni)

Islam (Shiite)

Buddhism

Hinduism

Chinese syncretism

Japanese syncretism

Catholic minorities    +

Judaism    ✳

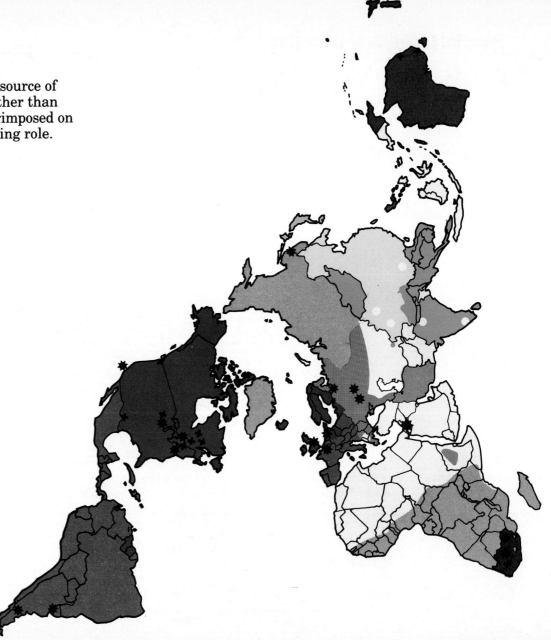

# Imperial Languages of the World

The criterion used to define an imperial language is the combination of its numerical importance *and* its geographic diffusion. In this respect Japanese is not imperial, and German since 1945 has lost its preponderance in Eastern Europe. Chinese (Peking Mandarin), although only partly meeting the criteria above, is still the most widely spoken language in the world.

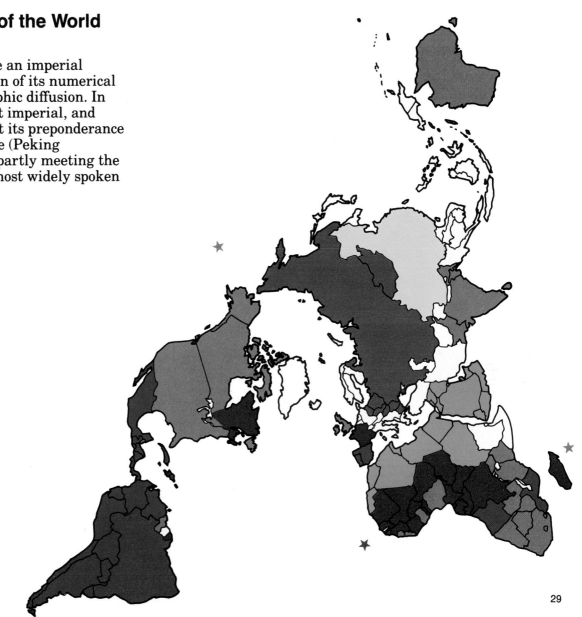

English
French
Spanish
Portuguese
Arabic
Russian
Chinese

# Enduring Traditional Enmities

The traditional enmities noted here are those
that still persist. Franco-German or
Anglo-French rivalry, for example, no longer
has a place here. Conversely, other enmities
based on ancient geohistorical rivalries
continue to revive latent tensions and, often
hidden behind ideological arguments, fuel
more or less open antagonisms.

↔ Interstate hostility

Serious interstate hostility

Inter-ethnic rivalry

Indian-white hostility

◣ Black/white dividing line

# Traditional Enmities*

## ASIA:

China–USSR
China–Vietnam
Vietnam–Khmers
Thailand–Burma
China–Mongols
India–Pakistan
Korea–Japan
Thailand–Cambodia

## MIDDLE EAST:

Although of recent origin, the enmity between the Arab countries and Israel has all the characteristics of a lasting rivalry.
Syria–Turkey (fueled by the claim to the *sanjak* of Alexandretta).

## AFRICA:

A north–south line through the Sahel divides the black African populations to the south and the Arab and Saharan populations to the north along an ancient cleavage based on slavery. See, for example, Chad, southern Sudan, and so on.

In the Horn of Africa: Ethiopia–Somalia (enmity formerly based on religious rivalry at the present time based on rival nationalisms).

In sub-Saharan Africa, ethnic rivalries are legion. Among those that have been particularly active: Tutsi–Hutu relations in Burundi and Rwanda, or the better-known case of the Ibo of Biafra.

In southern Africa, ethnic and tribal strategies play an important role. Angola: UNITA represents the Ovimbundu, who are opposed to the Luanda government, which rests on the alliance between the Kimbundu and the Bakongo. In Namibia, SWAPO is supported mainly by the Ovambo. In Zimbabwe, there is the rivalry between the Shona and the Ndebele, a source of conflict that could lead to civil war.

In South Africa, Pretoria uses and fosters tribal rivalries, especially between the Zulu and other ethnic groups.

## AMERICA:

Brazil–Argentina

Latin America–United States. (The resentment, arising from humiliation, of some groups in Latin America toward the United States is ambiguous to the extent that the interests of privileged strata, however nationalistic they may be, coincide with those of the United States.)

Indians–Hispanics (Peru, Ecuador, Bolivia, Guatemala, and so on).

## EUROPE:

Bulgaria–Turkey, Bulgaria–Yugoslavia
Greece–Turkey, Yugoslavia–Albania
USSR–Turkey
Romania–Hungary (claims relating to the Hungarians in Transylvania)
Poland–USSR
Poland–Germany

---

*Interstate enmities not including minority problems. This list is far from complete.

# THE HISTORICAL CONTEXT OF THE CONTEMPORARY WORLD

# Europeanization of the World at the Beginning of the Twentieth Century

In an uninterrupted process, the expansion of Europe from the sixteenth century onward resulted in the occupation by Europe of the whole of the American continent. During the nineteenth century and until after World War I, European imperialism extended its domination over the whole globe, with the partial exception of Japan. The global superiority of Europe in both technology and *ideas* was at the time total.

Europe

European population (dense)

European population (sparse)

European influence (semi-colonial)

European colonization

Japanese empire

# Territorial Changes in Europe Following the 1914–1918 War

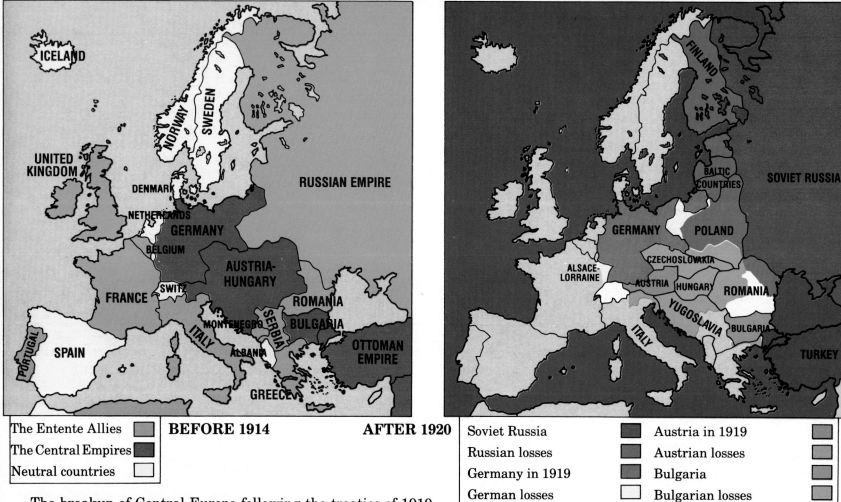

**BEFORE 1914**

- ICELAND
- UNITED KINGDOM
- NORWAY
- SWEDEN
- RUSSIAN EMPIRE
- DENMARK
- NETHERLANDS
- GERMANY
- BELGIUM
- AUSTRIA-HUNGARY
- FRANCE
- SWITZ
- ITALY
- MONTENEGRO
- SERBIA
- ROMANIA
- BULGARIA
- PORTUGAL
- SPAIN
- ALBANIA
- OTTOMAN EMPIRE
- GREECE

**AFTER 1920**

- FINLAND
- BALTIC COUNTRIES
- SOVIET RUSSIA
- GERMANY
- POLAND
- ALSACE-LORRAINE
- CZECHOSLOVAKIA
- AUSTRIA
- HUNGARY
- ROMANIA
- ITALY
- YUGOSLAVIA
- BULGARIA
- TURKEY

The Entente Allies
The Central Empires
Neutral countries

Soviet Russia
Russian losses
Germany in 1919
German losses
Austria in 1919
Austrian losses
Bulgaria
Bulgarian losses
Turkey

The breakup of Central Europe following the treaties of 1919–1920 ended traditional German influence in this area and resulted, among other things, in the formation of nation-states based on the ideas of Woodrow Wilson. These states were formed mostly at the expense of the Austro-Hungarian Empire and Russia. By 1945, with few exceptions, all the new states had become part of the Soviet sphere.

# The Colonial World between the Two World Wars

Although the states of Latin America were formally fully sovereign, the United States enjoyed almost total economic domination there. Similarly, the few formally independent states in Asia and Africa were often more like semi-colonies, with variations that must not be allowed to obscure their political autonomy.*

*The Union of South Africa became independent in 1910 and obtained a mandate over South-West Africa (Namibia) after World War I.

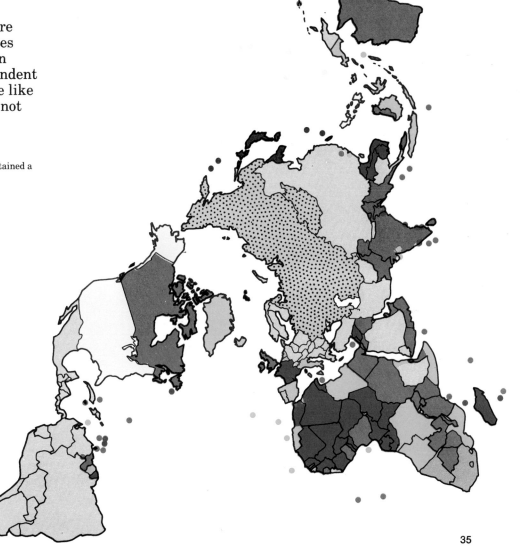

USA and possessions

UK and its empire

France and its empire

Other European nations and their colonies

Japan and its empire

USSR and Mongolia

Memel
1939

LITHUANIA

Danzig 1939

EAST PRUSSIA

Berlin ●

● Warsaw

GERMANY

POLAND

RHINELAND
(REMILITARIZED)

SUDETENLAND
1938

SAAR
(PLEBISCITE)

BOHEMIA
(GERMAN
PROTECTORATE)
1939

● Prague

Teschen 1939

MORAVIA

FRANCE

SLAVIC STATES
(INDEP. 1939)

(1939)

RUTHENIA

Munich ●

Vienna ●

Bratislava ●

AUSTRIA
(ANSCHLUSS) 1938

HUNGARY

SWITZERLAND

Budapest ●

**Expansion of the
Third Reich from
1933 to 1939**

Germany in 1933

German lands

German majority
regions

Slavic regions

Hungary before 1938

Hungarian
annexations

Polish annexations       ⊙

Czechoslovakia
before 1938

## Japanese Expansion, 1920–1940

| | |
|---|---|
| Japan in 1920 | ■ |
| Expansion 1937-39 | ■ |
| Protectorate 1932 | ■ |

## Italy's Colonial Expansion, 1920–1939

| | |
|---|---|
| Italy | ■ |
| Colonies 1920 | ■ |
| Conquests 1935-39 | ■ |

# Expansion of the Axis Powers between the Two World Wars

## GERMANY

- 1934—reunion of the Saar
- 1936—remilitarization of the Rhineland
- 1938 (March)—annexation of Austria
- 1938 (October)—annexation of the Sudetenland (Munich Conference)
- 1939 (March)—breakup of Czechoslovakia (annexation of Bohemia-Moravia)
- 1939 (March)—annexation of Memel (Lithuania)
- 1939 (September)—invasion of Poland

## ITALY

- 1924—annexation of the city of Fiume (Istria)
- 1935–1938—colonization of Cyrenaica (Libya)
- 1935–1936—conquest of Ethiopia
- 1939 (April)—invasion of Albania

## JAPAN

- 1931—occupation of Manchuria
- 1935—annexation of Chahar and Suiyuan (Chinese Mongolia)
- 1937–1939—occupation of northeast China, the lower Yangtse valley, and the southern coastal areas

37

# The World at War—1942

This map shows the territorial imbalance between the Axis Powers at the time of their greatest expansion (late 1942) and the Allies, their possessions, and the states sympathetic to them.

Allied nations

Favorable to Allies

Axis nations

Neutral

Maximum expansion
of Axis nations

## Europe after World War II

The USSR gained some 600,000 square kilometers in the west at the expense of Poland, the Baltic countries, Romania, Czechoslovakia, and Finland. In terms of square kilometers, it recovered exactly what Russia had lost by the Treaty of Brest-Litovsk (1918).

The great loser was Germany, divided into occupied zones and then into two states. The Cold War began in 1948 and froze this division. The Helsinki Accords (1976) formally confirmed Soviet domination in Eastern Europe.

| | | |
|---|---|---|
| USSR before the war | GREAT BRITAIN | |
| Soviet annexations | British occupation zones | |
| Soviet occupation zones | USA occupation zones | |
| Soviet influence | Other Western states, allies | |
| FRANCE | Neutral states | |
| French occupation zones | Iron Curtain (1947) | — |

## Germany 1945

Germany, which had an area of 540,000 sq. km. before 1914 and 474,000 sq. km. before 1938, was reduced to 248,000 sq. km. for the Federal German Republic and 108,000 sq. km. for the German Democratic Republic. Some 12 million Germans were expelled from various states in Central Europe and returned to occupied Germany. Between 1947 and 1961, some 4 million East Germans sought refuge in West Germany. For fifteen years the *Ostpolitik*, which accepts the fact of the division, has reflected the particular attitude of West Germany and of a large section of its public opinion toward problems of war and peace.

## Poland

Before 1939: 388,000 sq. km.
Today: 312,000 sq. km.
Six million Poles were deported and exterminated, including 3 million Jews. One million Poles were expelled from the eastern regions. The Soviet Union's territorial ambitions in the west led the Allies at Yalta (February 1945), and especially at Potsdam (July–August 1945), to compensate Poland for Russian annexation of the eastern Polish provinces by granting Poland Silesia and part of Pomerania and East Prussia.

East Berlin ▮
West Berlin ▮
Forests, parks ▮

Major arteries ——
Railways ——

**West Berlin, an Enclave in the East**

## West Berlin: An Anomaly

West Berlin, situated in the middle of the German Democratic Republic, 110 km. from West Germany, was for a long time (1947–1961) an abscess in the body of the Cold War. After the building of the wall by the GDR, the status quo gradually became stabilized.

### CHRONOLOGY:

**1949**—blockade of Berlin by the USSR; American airlift
**1961**—construction of the wall cutting off West Berlin and preventing the exodus of East Germans

**Links between West Berlin and West Germany**

FRG ▢
GDR ▮
Air corridors | | |
Railways ——
Main highways ——

**Defeated Japan in 1945**

Japan before 1945 ■
Lost territories □
Lost protectorates ▨

## Japan

The Japanese empire (630,000 sq. km., including 380,000 sq. km. for Japan proper) collapsed after the atomic bomb attacks on Hiroshima and Nagasaki in 1945. The USSR, which had declared war on Japan at the last moment, annexed strategic positions in the north of the archipelago in the Kuril Islands and the southern half of Sakhalin. China recovered its sovereignty over Manchuria and the island of Taiwan.

Japan was demilitarized and underwent a process of institutional democratization during the American occupation. In Micronesia, the United States secured trusteeship over the formerly Japanese island chains of the Marianas, the Carolines, and the Marshalls. In the late 1970s the United States handed back the Ryukyu archipelago (Okinawa). The Greater East Asia Co-Prosperity Sphere, envisaged militarily in the 1930s, appears to be becoming a reality today economically, although the impact of Japanese commercial penetration is worldwide.

# The West's Perception, at the Beginning of the Cold War (1948–1952), of Soviet and Communist Expansionism Worldwide

1945
★ Berlin (1949)
★ Czechoslovakia (1948)
1945
★ Greece (1947)
1949
Tibet (1950)
Korea (1950) ★
Indochina (1946) ★
Philippines (1949) ★
Malaysia (1948) ★

1946–1954—War in Indochina
1947–1949—Greek civil war
1948—Yugoslavian crisis
1948—Coup in Prague
1948–1957—Guerrillas in Malaysia
1948–1949—Blockade of Berlin
1949–1952—Huk guerrillas in the Philippines
1950—Invasion of Tibet
1950–1953—Korean war

USSR
Soviet annexations
USSR allies
Yugoslavia
Communist aggression ★

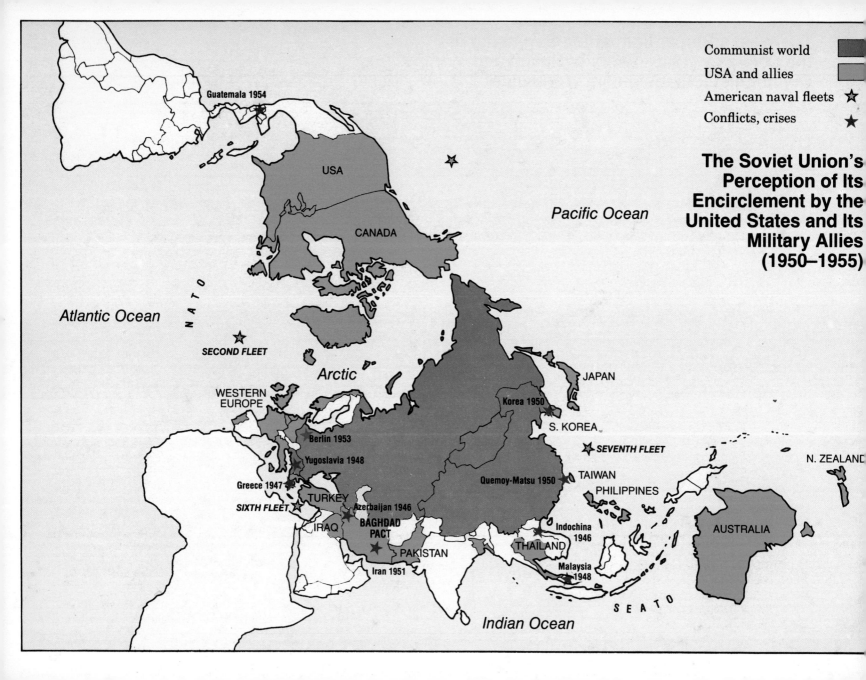

**The Soviet Union's Perception of Its Encirclement by the United States and Its Military Allies (1950–1955)**

Communist world
USA and allies
American naval fleets ☆
Conflicts, crises ★

Pacific Ocean

Atlantic Ocean

Arctic

NATO

USA

CANADA

Guatemala 1954

SECOND FLEET

WESTERN EUROPE

JAPAN

Korea 1950

S. KOREA

Berlin 1953

SEVENTH FLEET

Yugoslavia 1948

Greece 1947

TURKEY

Quemoy-Matsu 1950

TAIWAN

PHILIPPINES

N. ZEALAND

SIXTH FLEET

Azerbaijan 1946

BAGHDAD PACT

IRAQ

PAKISTAN

Indochina 1946

THAILAND

AUSTRALIA

Iran 1951

Malaysia 1948

SEATO

Indian Ocean

# Decolonization and the New States, 1945–1983

From the end of World War II, first in Asia and then a decade later in Africa, in a process that was at times violent, national liberation movements brought about the independence of over a hundred new states. Namibia (formerly South-West Africa) remains at present under South African rule.

Independent 1945

Independent since 1945

Dependent in 1983

Guyana (France)

Namibia (South Africa)

# Chronology of Decolonizations in Southeast Asia and in Africa

## THE NEAR EAST

| | Date of Independence |
|---|---|
| Yemen | 1918 |
| Saudi Arabia | 1926 |
| Iraq | 1932 |
| Jordan (Trans-Jordan) | 1946 |
| Libya, Syria | 1946 |
| Israel (partition of Palestine) | 1948 |

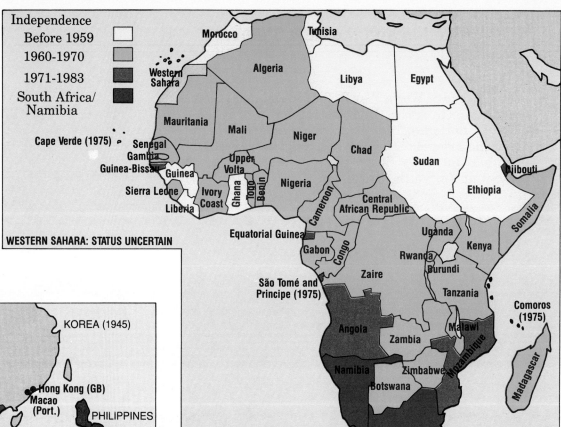

Independence
Before 1959
1960-1970
1971-1983
South Africa/Namibia

Cape Verde (1975)

Morocco
Tunisia
Western Sahara
Algeria
Libya
Egypt
Mauritania
Mali
Niger
Chad
Sudan
Senegal
Gambia
Guinea-Bissau
Guinea
Upper Volta
Sierra Leone
Ivory Coast
Ghana
Togo
Benin
Nigeria
Cameroon
Central African Republic
Ethiopia
Djibouti
Somalia
Liberia
Equatorial Guinea
Gabon
Congo
Zaire
Uganda
Kenya
Rwanda
Burundi
São Tomé and Principe (1975)
Tanzania
Comoros (1975)
Angola
Zambia
Malawi
Mozambique
Namibia
Zimbabwe
Madagascar
Botswana
South Africa

**WESTERN SAHARA: STATUS UNCERTAIN**

KOREA (1945)

PAKISTAN
BANGLA DESH
INDIA
BURMA
LAOS
Hong Kong (GB)
Macao (Port.)
PHILIPPINES
Bhandernagor (1954)
Goa (1963)
Yanam (1954)
VIETNAM
Mahé (1954)
Pondicherry (1954)
Karikal (1954)
CAMBODIA
SRI LANKA
MALAYSIA
Singapore
INDONESIA
TIMOR

Independence
Before 1950
Before 1960
After 1960

| | |
|---|---|
| Cyprus | 1960 |
| Kuwait | 1961 |
| South Yemen | 1967 |
| Oman, Bahrain, the Emirates | 1971 |

Several archipelagos and islands—and Guyana—in the Caribbean are not independent.

# Conflicts in the World since 1945

**Interstate Conflicts**

Legend:
- Contested waters
- Contested frontiers
- Secondary conflicts ■
- Major conflicts ●
- Limited interventions ▲

There have been over a hundred significant conflicts during the period 1945–1983.

To classify them, the following typology may be proposed:
- Interstate conflicts (conventional wars)
- Liberation wars (in a colonial context or one of foreign occupation)
- Internal conflicts (civil wars arising out of class, ethnic, and/or religious conflicts)

It is estimated that these conflicts have generated, in the period 1945–1982, some 13.5 million victims, an annual rate of about 350,000. (We do not deal here with the wave of terrorist attacks, whether trans-state or not, which are often a substitute for guerrilla warfare but cause a very limited number of victims. When this form of conflict is used as the sole means, it is more than anything else a matter of psychological warfare.)

Ten of these wars, not necessarily those that have had most impact on public opinion, have alone involved over 10 million victims, three-quarters of the total. These are the two Indochina wars (1946–1975), the Indo-Pakistan wars (1947–1949 and 1971 Bangladesh), the Korean war, the Algerian war, the civil war in Sudan, the massacres in Indonesia (1965), and the Biafran war.*

Many conflicts have resulted in significant numbers of refugees: Palestinians, subcontinental Indians, Indochinese, Ethiopians, Afghanis, Central Americans, and so on.

---

*Apart from wars and guerrilla wars, other types of political conflict have resulted in large numbers of victims. For example in Cambodia (1975–1978), in China during the Cultural Revolution, in Equatorial Guinea under Macias or in Uganda under Idi Amin Dada, in Argentina, in Rwanda (1960–1965), in Burundi (1972–1973), and so on.

# I. INTERSTATE CONFLICTS

A. MAJOR CONFLICTS:
India-Pakistan (1947–1949)
Arab-Israeli (1948–1949)
Korea (1950–1953)
Israel-Egypt (1956)
India-Pakistan (1965)
Vietnam (1965–1973)—massive intervention by the USA*
Arab-Israeli (1967)
India-Pakistan (1971)—Bangladesh
Arab-Israeli (1973)
Vietnam-China (1979)
Iran-Iraq (1980–    )
Great Britain-Argentina (1982)—Falkland Islands

B. SECONDARY CONFLICTS:
China-Taiwan (1950)—Quemoy-Matsu
China-Tibet (1950–1951)
Guatemala-Honduras (1954)—Operation CIA
India-China (1959)—Ladakh
Netherlands-Indonesia (1960–1962)—New Guinea
India-China (1962)—Assam
Indonesia-Malaysia (1963)—Sarawak, Borneo
Algeria-Morocco (1963)
China-USSR (1969)—Ussuri
Salvador-Honduras (1969)
Greece-Turkey (1974)—Cyprus
Syria-Lebanon (1976)—occupation
Indonesia-East Timor (1976)—annexation
  by Indonesia

---

*Air strikes in North Vietnam; civil war in South Vietnam.

Somalia-Ethiopia (1977–1978)
Vietnam-Cambodia (1978)
North Yemen-South Yemen (1979)
Israel-Lebanon (1982)—PLO

C. INTERVENTIONS:
Suez, French-British intervention (1956)
Budapest, Soviet intervention (1956)
Lebanon, U.S. intervention (1958)
Mauritania, French intervention (1961)
Cuba (1961)—Playa Girón
Bizerte, French intervention (1961)
Goa (Portuguese possession), Indian intervention (1961)
Zaire, Belgian intervention (1961 and 1964)
Gabon, French intervention (1964)
Uganda-Kenya-Tanzania, British intervention (1964)
Santo Domingo, U.S. intervention (1965)
Prague, Soviet intervention (1968)
Cambodia, U.S. intervention (1970)
Jordan, royal forces against the PLO (1970)
Angola, interventions by South Africa, Zaire, and especially Cuba (1975–1976)
Shaba (Zaire), French and Moroccan interventions (1977)
Djibouti, French intervention (1976–1977)
Ethiopia, Cuban intervention (1977)
Kolwezi (Zaire), French intervention (1978)
Chad, numerous interventions by French forces (1968–1980)
Uganda, Tanzanian intervention (1979)
Angola, South African interventions (1980, 1981, 1982)
Central Africa, French intervention (1979)
Chad, Libyan intervention (1980)

Gambia, Senegalese intervention (1980)
Chad, French intervention (1983)
Grenada, American intervention (1983)

Cambodia, against a regime put in place by Vietnam (1979–    )
Afghanistan, against the Soviet occupation (1979–    )

## II. LIBERATION MOVEMENTS FOR INDEPENDENCE DIRECTED AGAINST FOREIGN DOMINATION OR OCCUPATION

Palestine (Zionist movement), against Great Britain (1945–1947)
Indochina war (Vietnam), against France (1946–1954)
Laos (Pathet-Lao), against France (1946–1954)
Indonesia, against the Netherlands (1946–1949)
Malaysia, against Great Britain (1948–1957)
Kenya (Mau Mau insurrection), against Great Britain (1952–1954)
Tunisia, against France (1952–1956)
Morocco, against France (1953–1956)
Algeria, against France (1954–1962)
Cyprus, against Great Britain (1955–1959)
Cameroon, against France (1957–1960)
Belgian Congo (1958–1960)
Angola, against Portugal (1961–1974)
South Yemen, against Great Britain (1963–1967)
Guinea-Bissau, against Portugal (1963–1974)
Palestinians, against Israel, especially since 1967 (1965–    )
Mozambique, against Portugal (1964–1974)
Namibia, against South Africa (1970–    )
Rhodesia/Zimbabwe, against white Rhodesian domination (1972–1979)
East Timor, against Indonesia (1974–    )
Western Sahara, against Morocco (1975–    )

## III. CONFLICTS OVER SECESSION* OR TO GAIN AUTONOMY WITHIN ESTABLISHED STATES

Azerbaijan and the Kurdish republic of Mahabad, Iran (1946)
Burma (Karens, etc.) (1948–1954)
Hyderábad, resistance to incorporation into India (1948)
South Moluccas (1950–1952)
Tibet, against China (1955–1959)
Katanga (Zaïre) (1960–1964)
Kurds, in Iraq (1961–1970, 1974–1975, 1979–    )
Eritrea, Ethiopia (1961–    )
South Sudan (1966–1972, 1982–    )
Biafra, Nigeria (1967–1970)
India (Nagas) (1967–1970)
Baluchistan (Pakistan) (1973–1977)
Ogaden (Ethiopia) (1974–    )
Basques in Spain (1975–1981)
Philippine Muslims (1977–    )
Kurds in Iran (1978–    )

---

*As in civil wars (IV), the date of the beginning of the operations is often uncertain.

## IV. CIVIL WARS FOUGHT TO CHANGE REGIMES*

China (1945–1949)
Greece (1947–1949)
Huks (Philippines) (1949–1952)
Colombia, chronic upheaval (1953)
Cuba (1956–1959)
South Vietnam (1957–1964; 1973–1975)
Sumatra, insurrection against the centrist regime of Jakarta (1957–1958)
Zaire (1960–1965)
Malaysia, (sporadic)
Laos (1960–1975)
Thailand (sporadic)
Cameroon (1960–1966)
Guatemala (1961–1968; 1980–    )
Venezuela (1962–1967)
Yemen, with Egyptian intervention (1962–1967)
Rwanda (1963–1964)
Cyprus, intervention by the U.N. (1963–1964)
Cambodia (1965–1975)
Indonesia (1965)
Uruguay (1965–1973)
Peru (1965, and 1982–    )
Bolivia (1967)
Brazil (1967–1970)
Northern Ireland (Catholics) (1968–    )
Chad (1968–1982)
Dhofar, in Oman, with intervention by Great Britain, Iran, and Jordan (1968–1976)
Nicaragua, (1972–1979)
Burundi (1972)
Chile, military repression (1973)
Argentina (1973–1977)
Lebanon, chronic upheaval (1975–1977)
Angola (UNITA), with the aid of South Africa (1976–    )

El Salvador (1976–    )
Iran (1978–1979)
Afghanistan (1978–1979)
Mozambique (FMN), with the aid of South Africa (1980–    )
Philippines (1980–    )

**Internal Conflicts**

Secessionist conflicts ▲
Wars of liberation ●
Civil wars ■

*For all intents and purposes, all such conflicts since 1945 have taken place in the Third World.

# A WORLD OF OCEANS

Arctic Ocean

Atlantic Ocean

Indian Ocean

Pacific Ocean

EQUATOR

1 French nautical mile = 1,852 km.
1 English nautical mile = 1,855 km.
1 U.S. nautical mile = 1,853.25 km.

**Total surface of the world**—510 million sq. km.
**Land surface**—149 million sq. km. (29%)
**Covered by water**—361 million sq. km. (71%)

**Ocean surfaces**
Pacific Ocean—161.7 million sq. km.
Atlantic Ocean—81.6 million sq. km.
Indian Ocean—73.4 million sq. km.
Arctic Ocean—14.3 million sq. km.

# Military Dispositions around the Arctic

The Arctic separates the USSR and the United States. Control of the surface of this ocean and its air space is of vital importance. Beneath the frozen stretches of sea there has developed, with nuclear submarines, a subglacial theater of operations of equally vital strategic importance.

**Legend:**

- U.S. and NATO bases ✳
- Soviet bases ★
- Distances ←
- Claims of sovereignty ---
- Contested area (USSR-Norway) ▨
- Svalbard area
- Permanent ice cap
- Seasonal ice
- Open waters

Pacific Ocean
Atlantic Ocean

KISKA
ADAK
SHEMYA
UNALASKA
Aleutians
PRIBILOV
UM KAMTCHASK
PETROPAVLOVSK
SOV GAVAN
JAPAN
KODIAK
KAMCHATKA
NIKOLAYEVSK
VLADIVOSTOK
5000 km
ANCHORAGE
NOME
ANADYR
PROVIDENIYA
MAGADAN
OKHOTSK
VICTORIA
VANCOUVER
BERING STRAIT
MAC CHORD
FAIRBANKS
KOTZEBUE
PEVEK
AMBARTCHIK
YAKOUTSK
USA
MALMSTROM
CANADA
BARROW
6000 km
EDMONTON
Beaufort Sea
Sea
TIKSI
MINOT
SAWYER
Laptev
NORDVIK
USSR
G. FORKS
6500 km
WINNIPEG
CHURCHILL
NORILSK
NORTH POLE
DIKSON
Hudson Bay
THULE
4500 km
Barents Sea
NOVOSIBIRSK
6500 km
Frobisher Bay
4500 km
Novaya Zemlya
VORKOUTA
QUEBEC
Baffin Bay
GREENLAND
6500 m
Svalbards
SVERDLOVSK
LORING
SONDRE
MURMANSK
Kola
ARKHANGELSK
HALIFAX
Strait of Denmark
Sea of Norway
NARVII
ARGENTIA
KEYFLAVIK
LENINGRAD
ICELAND
NORWAY
MOSCOW
Faeroes
STOCKHOLM
OSLO
GREAT BRITAIN
HOLY LOCH

# The Arctic: Communications

The Arctic is not well-suited to navigation. With the ports of Murmansk and Archangel, the USSR has a relatively favorable position there.

The Faeroe Islands and the Strait of Denmark, outlets to the Atlantic, are easy to watch. Arctic air space is regularly used by several international airlines.

Pacific Ocean
Atlantic Ocean
Sea of Okhotsk
Beaufort Sea
Barents Sea
Hudson Bay
Baffin Bay
Probisher Bay
Denmark Strait
North Pole

JAPAN
VLADIVOSTOK
PETROPAVLOVSK
NIKOLAYEVSK
ALEUTIANS
UM KAMTCHASK
KAMCHATKA
PRIBILOV
ANADYR
MAGADAN
AMBARTCHIK
ANCHORAGE
FAIRBANKS
PEVEK
YAKOUTSK
VANCOUVER
ALASKA
TIKSI
USA
CANADA
EDMONTON
Lena
NORDVIK
VICTORIA
NORILSK
DIKSON
WINNIPEG
CHURCHILL
USSR
ELLESMERE
NOVOSIBIRSK
Ob
VORKOUTA
QUEBEC
GREENLAND
SVALBARDS
SVERDLOVSK
Ienissei
HALIFAX
GODTHAB
MURMANSK
KOLA
ARKHANGELSK
NARVIK
LENINGRAD
MOSCOW
REYKJAVIK
ICELAND
FAEROES
NORWAY
STOCKHOLM
OSLO
GREAT BRITAIN
GLASGOW

Bering Strait
NEW YORK-JAPAN
Convention of 1867
COPENHAGEN-JAPAN
LONDON-VANCOUVER
LOS ANGELES-COPENHAGEN
MOSCOW-JAPAN
Accord of 1973
Treaty of 1920

**Legend:**

| | |
|---|---|
| Air routes | ——— |
| Claims of sovereignty | - - - |
| Contested area | ▨ |
| Svalbard Is. area | ⌐¬ |
| Permanent ice cap | ⬜ |
| Seasonal ice | ⬜ |
| Open waters | ⬛ |

# The Bering Strait

Permanent ice cap

Icebound (6-9 months)

Open water

Iceberg zones

USA and allies

USSR and allies

Soviet radar system

Arctic sea lane

NATO radar system

U.S. and Allied bases ✳

U.S. support points ●

Soviet bases ★

Soviet support points ■

Iron ore ◆

Other mineral ores ▼

Airfields ⊕

Distances in nautical miles

Arctic Ocean

CANADA

P. Barrow

WRANGEL I.

ALASKA

Fairbanks

Yakoutsk

USSR

Ambartchik

600 Miles

Kotzebue

Nome

Anchorage

Anadyr

ST. LAWRENCE

Kodiak

Okhotsk

Magadan

Sea of Okhotsk

PRIBILOF IS.

Nikolayevsk

KOMANDORSKIYE IS.

Unalaska

SAKHALIN

170 miles

ALEUTIANS

Adak

Vladivostok

Petropavlovsk

Shemya

Kiska

Pacific Ocean

Sov. Gavan

## North Cape Passage

GREAT BRITAIN

Keflavik

GREENLAND

Holy Loch

220 m

150 m

ICELAND

FAEROES

MAYEN I.

Shetland

NORWAY

SVALBARDS

240 m

120 m

SWEDEN

Narvik

30 m

Baltisk

FINLAND

Severomorsk

Murmansk

Riga

Leningrad

USSR

Arkhangelsk

Belioucha

## Kola Peninsula

Barents Sea

CAPE KANIN

NORTH CAPE

Varanger Fjord

Motovskiy Bay

Pechenga

Severomorsk

Mezen

FINMARK

Poljarny

Kirkenes

Murmansk

Nikel

U S S R

Monchegorsk

KOLA PENINSULA

Apatity

NORWAY

SWEDEN

White Sea

Arkhangelsk

FINLAND

Severodinsk

Kiruna

# Outlets from the Arctic

Since the early 1920s, the coastal states have pushed the limits of their territorial waters well beyond those then accepted. There is a dispute between the USSR and Norway about this covering an area of 150,000 sq. km. around the Svalbard Islands. By the Treaty of Paris (1920), 41 signatory states (including the USSR) share equal rights to mine coal in the Svalbard Islands—which, however, remain under Norwegian authority.

## TOWARD THE ATLANTIC

This access route is essential to the northern Soviet fleet based in the region of Murmansk and the White Sea. The polar basin between Greenland and the Svalbard Islands (Spitsbergen) is icebound most of the time and is difficult to navigate. The Barents Sea between North Cape and the Svalbard Islands is the only passage in open waters. Norway's position at North Cape is strategically vital, but highly vulnerable.

## TOWARD THE PACIFIC

The Bering Strait (40 miles) is also icebound for more than six months a year. Its narrowness and shallowness (about 40 m.) make it easy to watch and blockade. Farther south, the string of the Aleutian (USA) and the Komandorskie islands (USSR) complete control of this outlet from the Arctic toward the Pacific.

## THE NORTHERN SEA ROUTE

This route is open two or three months a year and makes it easier for the USSR to develop northern Siberia, and provides a shorter sea route between Murmansk and Vladivostok. There is no similar route open along the northern coasts of Canada. Only seasonal navigation is possible in Hudson Bay and the Baffin Sea.

# Alaska

Alaska, the poleward extension of the United States, (1.5 million sq. km. and 400,000 inhabitants) is of major strategic significance and contains large reserves of oil and natural gas. Anchorage is heavily used by transpolar airlines.

**Outlets**

*Barents Channel:*
    North Cape → 280 NM ← Ours I. → 120 NM → Svalbard Is.

*Denmark Strait:* 150 NM
    Greenland → Svalbard: 240 NM
    Iceland → Faeroe Is.: 200 NM
    Faeroe Is. → Shetland Is.: 150 NM

**Distances**
    Bering Strait ↔ Denmark Strait: 3,000 NM
    Bering ↔ Murmansk (northern sea route): 3,800 NM

NM: Nautical miles.

**The Arctic: Enormous Resources, Difficult to Exploit**

# The Atlantic: A Western Ocean

The North Atlantic is the "inner sea" of the Euro-American world and the countries in its geopolitical orbit.

In the absence of any coastal maritime power, the South Atlantic remains an area essentially controlled by Europe and the United States.

Except for Iceland and the Cape Verde islands, the islands in the sea are all still under the control of Great Britain and other NATO countries.

The Canaries, Madeira, and especially the Azores are valuable staging points in the North Atlantic.

The USSR, whose fleet has grown considerably, was for a long time not present on this ocean, but today it has access to facilities, especially in Cuba and Angola.

## Map

GREENLAND
ICELAND
CANADA
UNITED KINGDOM
FRG
FRANCE
3570 nm
UNITED STATES
NEW YORK
3150 nm
PORTUGAL
SPAIN
Mediterranean
Azores (Port.)
Str. of Gibraltar
Bermuda (UK)
Madeira (Port.)
6800 nm
MEXICO
Canary Is. (Sp.)
CUBA
2000 nm
Puerto Rico (US)
Cape Verde Is.
DAKAR
Caribbean
Antilles
NICARAGUA
PANAMA
VENEZUELA
NIGERIA
4800 nm
1750 nm
EQUAT. GUINEA
S. TOMÉ
F. De Noronha (BR)
BRAZIL
Ascension (UK)
ANGOLA
6200 nm
St. Helena (UK)
Pacific Ocean
3300 nm
SOUTH AFRICA
ARGENTINA
THE CAPE
2400 nm
Tristan da Cunha (UK)
Gough (UK)
Falklands (UK)
South Georgia (UK)

### Legend

- Pro-Soviet states
- USA and NATO members
- Other Western allies
- European neutrals
- African states
- Latin American states
- Frozen in winter
- 200-mile limit
- U.S. and NATO bases ★
- Soviet bases ✳
- Distances ——

# The Atlantic Ocean: An Economic Crossroads

The main industrial areas of North America and Western Europe remain heavily dependent on supplies of raw materials that come via the Atlantic. The security of sea routes and the various key access points is thus vital for the Western powers.

In terms of the tonnage transported and the number of ships using it, the Atlantic is the busiest ocean. Similarly, North Atlantic air space has the heaviest commercial aviation traffic.

## The Busiest Ocean

| RESOURCES AND ACTIVITIES | |
|---|---|
| Industrial regions | |
| Petroleum | ▲ |
| Uranium | ● |
| Coal | ■ |
| Mineral ore | ✳ |
| Major ports | ● |
| Sea lanes | ══ |
| Frozen in winter | ☐ |
| 200-mile limit | |

Hudson Bay, Seasonal route, Montreal, NORTHEAST GREAT LAKES, Boston, New York, New Orleans, BERMUDA, PUERTO RICO, Western USA, Colon, Panama Canal, ANTILLES, Maracaibo, Peru, FERNANDO DE NORONHA, Salvador, BRAZILIAN TRIANGLE, Rio, Santos, Buenos Aires, Chile, FALKLANDS, Str. of Magellan

Oslo, Rotterdam, London, Hamburg, NORTHWEST EUROPE, Bilbao, Lisbon, Genoa, AZORES, Gibraltar, MADEIRA, Casablanca, CANARY IS., CAPE VERDE, Dakar, Abidjan, Lagos, EQUAT. GUINEA, S. TOMÉ, ASCENSION, Luanda, ST. HELENA, Asia-Near East, Capetown, TR. DA CUNHA, GOUGH, S. GEORGIA

## The Two Mediterrraneans

**Legend:**
- Western allies
- USSR and pro-Soviet
- Other socialist nations
- Oil and natural gas ▲
- Soviet naval bases ■
- U.S. and Allied naval bases ■
- Mediterranean outlets ★

## THE MEDITERRANEAN

Since 1945, the strategic importance the Mediterranean had during the period of European hegemony has rapidly declined. Decolonization and the Arab–Israeli conflicts, which led on several occasions to the closure of the Suez Canal, have considerably reduced the level of its commercial activity. The main route for petroleum products today is around South Africa. Militarily, long-range strategic weapons have transformed this easily blockaded sea into a trap for fleets.

The role of the Mediterranean has become regional, even though at present the conflict in the Middle East and the upkeep of NATO's military forces in Italy, Greece, and Turkey require the presence of naval forces. Since its disengagement from Egypt, the USSR now has only one staging area—in Syria.

## THE CARIBBEAN BASIN

The Caribbean forms an "American Mediterranean." Traditionally, the United States has perceived this area as strategically vital, and it has numerous bases there, the main ones being at Panama, in the Canal Zone, in Puerto Rico, and at Guantanamo (Cuba). In the past, and recently, the United States has frequently intervened militarily in Central America and the Caribbean.

Compared to North and South America, the proliferation of ministates and the large number of small islands (a minority of which are not independent) make this area particularly vulnerable. In the last twenty years, more than a dozen new states have won independence. Since it was built, the Panama Canal has been primarily a passageway between the east and west coasts of the United States.

The Caribbean basin, dominated by the United States (except for Cuba, which appears as a troublemaker), is important for its oil and as a communications nexus. It has recently seen the emergence of two regional powers, Venezuela and Mexico. The states in this basin have been benefiting from favorable economic conditions assured by the United States, as well as from the low oil prices granted them by Venezuela and Mexico. Miami has become the real center of the Caribbean basin.

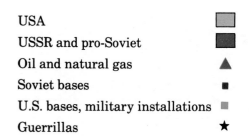

USA ▇

USSR and pro-Soviet ▇

Oil and natural gas ▲

Soviet bases ▪

U.S. bases, military installations ▪

Guerrillas ★

# The Indian Ocean

## A MAJOR AREA OF CONFLICT

Because of the flow of petroleum from the Persian Gulf and the instability or fragility of many of the coastal states, the Indian Ocean is potentially a major area of conflict.

From its important base on Diego Garcia, the United States is endeavoring, with its allies (Great Britain, France, etc.), to organize an operational strike force in this sensitive area. In addition to the 32 American ships, there are some 30 British vessels. France has 7 warships at Djibouti.

Since 1970, the deployment of Soviet forces, especially naval forces, has increased considerably. In Ethiopia and in South Yemen, and on Socotra, among others, the USSR has been able to obtain bases or well-sited facilities: 29 Soviet vessels now operate in the Indian Ocean.

Today, Suez and the Red Sea have ceased to be the main communication route to Europe and the Atlantic. But the Strait of Hormuz remains vital. Since 1967, tankers have carried oil by the Cape route—which enhances the already great strategic importance of southern Africa, where the Soviet Union gained a foothold in 1975 in Mozambique.

No coastal state, not even Australia or India, has sufficient sea power to play a role. The United States remains, with the support notably of Great Britain and France, the guarantor of the status quo.

Toward eastern Asia and Japan, ships use the two traditional routes through the Strait of Malacca and the Strait of Sunda* and, increasingly, the Strait of Lombok, because of its depth.

---

*The distance from the Persian Gulf to Japan is 6,500 miles by the first route and 7,500 miles by the second.

IRAQ
ISRAEL
IRAN
KUWAIT
AFGHANISTAN
EGYPT
SAUDI ARABIA
PAKISTAN
Persian Gulf
CHINA
Karachi
BANGLADESH
INDIA
Calcutta
Chittagong
YEMEN
Bombay
BURMA
S. YEMEN
OMAN
1980 nm
Rangoon
SUDAN
DJIBOUTI
Aden
SOCOTRA
Vishakhapatnam
THAILAND
VIETNAM
Berbera
Madras
ETHIOPIA
ANDAMAN IS.
Strait of Malacca
MALAYSIA
SINGAPORE
5250 nm
MALDIVES
Mogadiscio
3630 nm
Colombo
KENYA
3850 nm
4500 nm
Strait of Sunda
Mombasa
SEYCHELLES
DIEGO
GARCIA
Ocean
INDONESIA
TANZANIA
Dar Es Salaam
COMOROS
COCOS (AUST.)
Strait of Lombok
5600 nm
4900 nm
MOZAMBIQUE
Strait of Mozambique
MADAGASCAR
Tamatave
MAURITIUS
Indian
Beira
RÉUNION (FR.)
5460 nm

Indian diaspora + 100,000
AUSTRALIA
Maputo
− 100,000
SOUTH
AFRICA
Durban
Oil and natural gas
Mineral ores
Perth
Freemantle
P. Elizabeth
4750 nm
AMSTERDAM (FR.)
Industrialized zones
Capetown

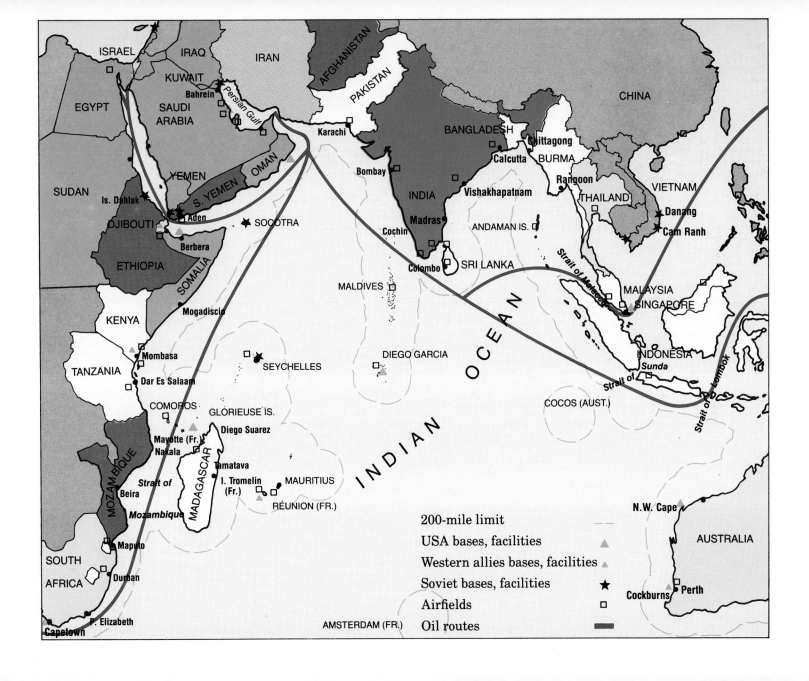

ISRAEL    IRAQ    IRAN
EGYPT    KUWAIT
        Bahrein
SAUDI
ARABIA          Persian Gulf          AFGHANISTAN
                                      PAKISTAN          CHINA
                        Karachi
SUDAN   YEMEN                                  BANGLADESH   Chittagong
        S. YEMEN  OMAN          Bombay              Calcutta   BURMA
Is. Dahlak                                                    Rangoon   VIETNAM
DJIBOUTI  Aden   SOCOTRA              INDIA    Vishakhapatnam   THAILAND   Danang
        Berbera              Cochin   Madras   ANDAMAN IS.              Cam Ranh
ETHIOPIA        SOMALIA                        SRI LANKA
KENYA           Mogadiscio   Colombo                          Strait of Malacca
TANZANIA        Mombasa              MALDIVES                  MALAYSIA
                                                              SINGAPORE
        Dar Es Salaam                DIEGO GARCIA
        COMOROS   SEYCHELLES                                  INDONESIA
                GLORIEUSE IS.                                 Sunda
        Mayotte (Fr.)   Diego Suarez                          Strait of
        Nakala                                    COCOS (AUST.)   Strait of Lombok
MOZAMBIQUE  MADAGASCAR  Tamatava              INDIAN  OCEAN
        I. Tromelin
Strait of  (Fr.)   MAURITIUS
Beira                                                         N.W. Cape
Mozambique        RÉUNION (FR.)
        Maputo                                                AUSTRALIA
SOUTH
AFRICA   Durban                    200-mile limit
                                   USA bases, facilities
        P. Elizabeth               Western allies bases, facilities
Capetown                           Soviet bases, facilities
                    AMSTERDAM (FR.)   Airfields              Cockburns   Perth
                                   Oil routes

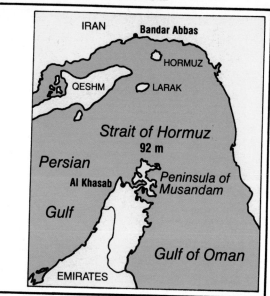

## The Persian Gulf and the Strait of Hormuz

**First map (Persian Gulf):**

IRAQ
Basra
Abadan
Bandar e Mashur
Khorramshahr
Umm Qasr
BUBIYAN
KUWAIT
IRAN
Busheher
Persian
Gulf
Ras Tannurah
LAVAN
QEYS
QESHM
Bandar Abbas
Strait of Hormuz
Ad Dammam
BAHRAIN
SAUDI ARABIA
QATAR
Doha
Abu Dhabi
Dubai
Fujairah
Indian
Ocean
Sohar
UNITED ARAB EMIRATES
OMAN

**Inset map (Strait of Hormuz):**

IRAN
Bandar Abbas
HORMUZ
QESHM
LARAK
Strait of Hormuz
92 m
Persian
Gulf
Al Khasab
Peninsula of Musandam
Gulf of Oman
EMIRATES

## Outlets from the Indian Ocean

## The Straits of Indonesia

China Sea
BORNEO
Java Sea
MALAYSIA
Singapore
INDONESIA
Strait of Malacca
SUMATRA
Surabaya
JAVA
Strait of Lombok
Strait of Sunda
Jakarta
Bandung
Indian Ocean
N

# RED SEA

**The Outlet toward Europe:
The Red Sea**

*diterranean*

ISRAEL

**Tel Aviv**
**Jerusalem**
● **Amman**

*andria*

JORDAN

**Port Said**
**Ismailiya**
**Suez**

*iro*

● **Elat**

● **Tabuk**

GYPT

SAUDI ARABIA

*Lake Aswan*

*Red*

**Jiddah**
● **Mecca**

*Sea*

SUDAN

**Dahlak**

**Asmera** ●

**Sana** ●

YEMEN

ETHIOPIA

**Assab**

S. YEMEN

**Aden**

*Gulf of*
*Aden*

**Djibouti**

**Berbera**

## THE STRAIT OF TIRAN

*Gulf of*
*Aqaba*

SAUDI
ARABIA

SINAI

*Strait of Tiran*

**TIRAN**

**SINAFIR**

**Sharm el Sheikh**

*Red Sea*

*Red Sea*

YEMEN

ETHIOPIA

S.
YEMEN

**PERIM**

*Bab el*
*Mandab*

*Gulf of*
*Aden*

DJIBOUTI

**DJEZIRET SOBA**

## THE STRAIT OF
## BAB EL MANDEB

*Mediterranean*

*MANZALA*

**Port Said**

● **El Kamtara**

**Ismailiya**

*TIMSAH*

*GREAT*
*BITTER LAKE*

*LITTLE*
*BITTER*
*LAKE*

**Suez**

*Red Sea*

## THE SUEZ CANAL

**Ain Sukhna**

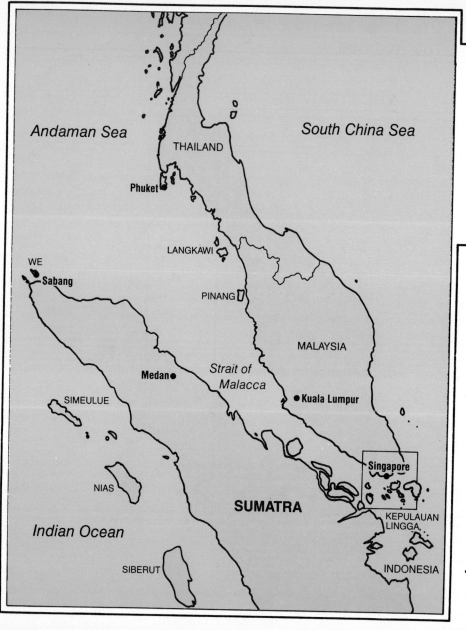

Andaman Sea

South China Sea

THAILAND

Phuket

LANGKAWI

WE
Sabang

PINANG

MALAYSIA

Strait of
Malacca

Medan

Kuala Lumpur

SIMEULUE

Singapore

NIAS

SUMATRA

KEPULAUAN
LINGGA

Indian Ocean

SIBERUT

INDONESIA

Johor Baharu

Singapore

KARIMUN     BATAM     BINTAN

KUNDUR

KEPULAUAN RIAU

## Singapore

Singapore remains one of the key points in Southeast Asia, both strategically and economically.

## The Strait of Malacca

## Disputed Areas in the South China Sea

In this region, there remain unresolved problems of sovereignty over parts of the continental shelf. In the northeast, the Chinese and Vietnamese are in dispute over the Paracel Islands, which have been occupied by the Chinese since the mid-1970s. In the south, Indonesia, the Philippines, Taiwan, and Vietnam all seek to assert their sovereignty over the Spratly Islands. Vietnam and Indonesia are in dispute over the continental shelf. In the Gulf of Thailand, Vietnam, Cambodia, and Thailand are in dispute.

CHINA · Canton · TAIWAN · Hong Kong · Haiphong · LAOS · Hainan · THAILAND · PARACEL IS. · Bangkok · VIETNAM · CAMBODIA · Gulf of Thailand · PHILIPPINES · Luzon · Manila · Phan Rang (Cam Ranh) · Ho Chi Minh (Saigon) · THE PALAUAN · SPRATLY IS. · South China Sea · 620 naut. mi. · 1700 naut. mi. · BUNGURAN IS. · MALAYSIA · Singapore · Sumatra · Borneo · INDONESIA · Jakarta · Java

**Legend:**

- USSR and pro-Soviet
- Western allies
- Contested waters

67

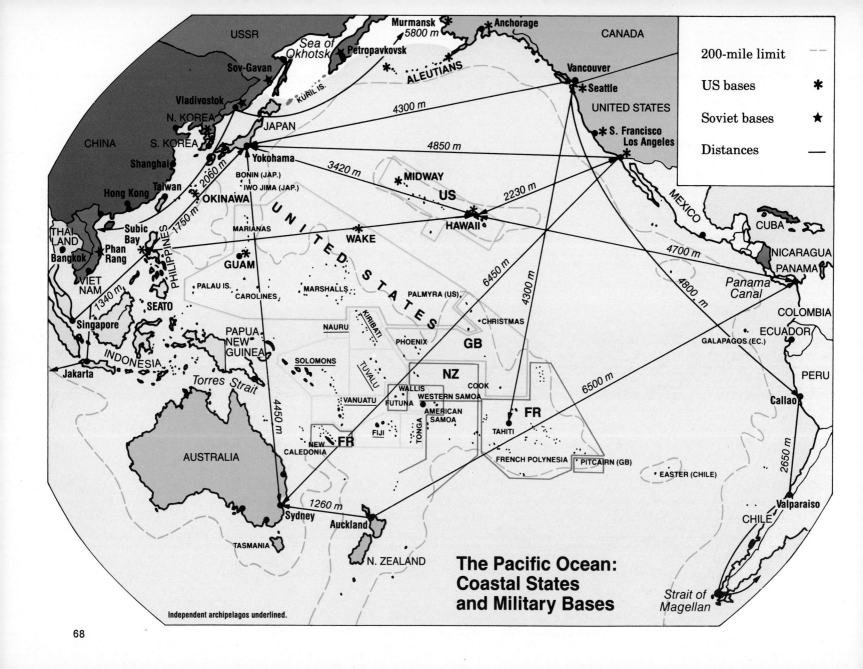

**The Pacific Ocean: Coastal States and Military Bases**

Independent archipelagos underlined.

Legend:
- 200-mile limit — – – –
- US bases — *
- Soviet bases — ★
- Distances — —

**Industrial Resources and Trade Routes**

US bases ✳
Soviet bases ★
200-mile limit
Major sea lanes
Industrialized regions
Coal **C**    Iron ◆
Petroleum **P**   Copper ■
Uranium **U**   Bauxite ●
Ores ✚

USSR
Murmansk ✳
Anchorage ✳
Bering Sea
Sea of Okhotsk
Petropavlovsk ★
CANADA
P
Vancouver ✳
Japan-Canada
C C
C C
Vladivostok ★
Tientsin
C
Yokohama
S. Francisco ✳
Pusan ★
Japan-USA
Shanghai
CHINA
Taipei
Los Angeles
P ✳
Canton ✚
Japan-Panama
Haiphong
Honolulu ✳
Hong Kong
✳
MEXICO
✳
Acapulco
Bangkok
Manila ★
GUAM (USA) ✳
P
USA-Europe
Ho Chi Minh
Truk (Carolinas)
Strait of Malacca
Singapore
Australia-Japan
Australia-USA
Panama
P P
Strait of Makassar
Strait of Sunda
P P
Jakarta
Strait of Lombok
Guyaquil
P
Port Moresby
Torres Strait
Coral Sea
Australia-Panama
Callao
Apia
AUSTRALIA
U
Noumea
Suva
Papeete
Brisbane
Japan-Asia, Europe, Middle East
Sydney
Adelaide
Melbourne
Valparaiso
Punta Arenas
Strait of Magellan
Europe-Middle East, The Cape

69

## The Pacific Ocean

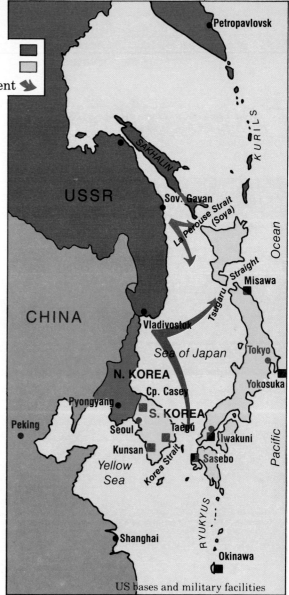

USSR and pro-Soviet
Western allies
Soviet naval deployment

Before World War II, the great powers showed little interest in this vast ocean. Their maritime activities were concentrated for the most part in the southwestern Pacific, and the ocean was merely a secondary highway.

With its seaboard on the Pacific, only the United States has, since the nineteenth century, pursued a coherent expansionist policy through the archipelagos to the Philippines. During World War II, Japan saw its imperial plans thwarted. Today, under the pressure of political changes that have occurred since 1945 in China and Southeast Asia, the role of the Pacific has grown. The economic importance of Japan and the growth of various states have intensified trade flows.

However, the Pacific has not yet become a new center of gravity, equal to the Atlantic. The continued preponderance of the Atlantic derives from the economic importance of Europe and the fact that both sides of that ocean are peopled by those sharing common origins and a common culture.

Control of Sakhalin and the Kuril Islands (formerly Japanese possessions) is important for the USSR. On its Pacific coast, only a small part of which is open to navigation throughout the year, the Japanese straits form so many gates opposite Vladivostok. Petropavlovsk, at the extreme tip of the Kamchatka, is icebound three or four months of the year.

In the Pacific, the USSR had no base until 1979. Since then, it has used Cam Ranh Bay in Vietnam, which is both a base and a communications center. Naval—and air—facilities also exist at Da Nang in Vietnam (see page 67).

**The Japanese Gates**

## Hawaii: Key Position in the Pacific

Most of the islands in the Pacific are under the trusteeship of the West and its allies (USA, Great Britain, France, New Zealand, Australia, Japan). U.S. hegemony is almost total in the northern Pacific. The central position of Hawaii, as base and as staging area, is vital in this arrangement.

The archipelago contains the major base of Pearl Harbor, which acts as support base for the Pacific fleet, and Camp Nimitz, the seat of the Armed Forces Pacific Command, and it is also a major air traffic center.

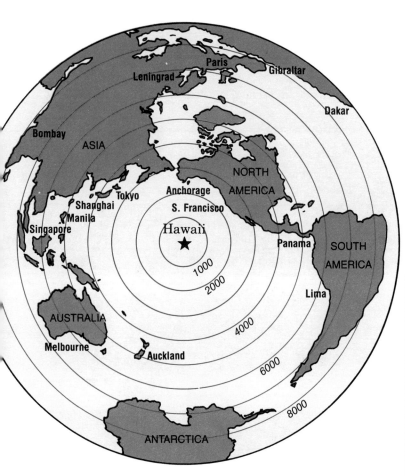

## Hawaii: The Fiftieth American State

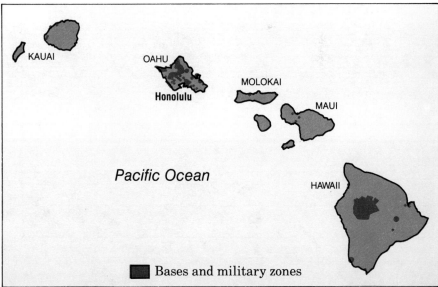

■ Bases and military zones

## Territorial Claims

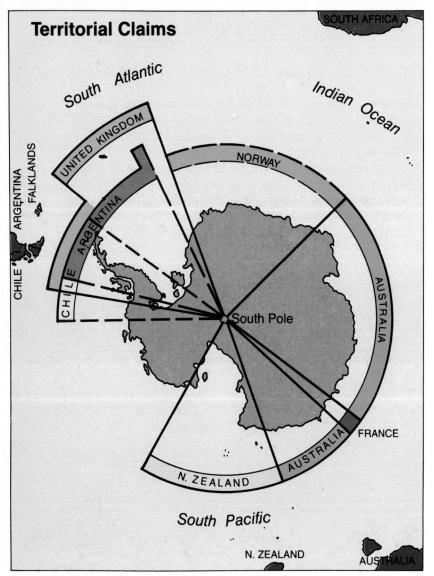

SOUTH AFRICA

South Atlantic

Indian Ocean

UNITED KINGDOM

NORWAY

ARGENTINA

FALKLANDS

CHILE

CHILE ARGENTINA

AUSTRALIA

South Pole

FRANCE

AUSTRALIA

N. ZEALAND

South Pacific

N. ZEALAND

AUSTRALIA

## Effective Presence

### SCIENTIFIC BASES

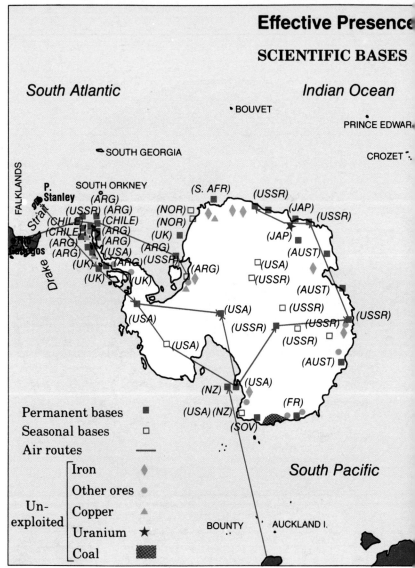

South Atlantic

Indian Ocean

BOUVET

PRINCE EDWARD

SOUTH GEORGIA

CROZET

FALKLANDS

P. Stanley

SOUTH ORKNEY

(ARG)

(S. AFR)

(USSR)

(USSR) (ARG)

(NOR)

(JAP)

(USSR)

(CHILE)

(CHILE)

(NOR)

(JAP)

(ARG)

(UK)

(AUST)

(CHILE)

(ARG)

(ARG)

(ARG)

(USA)

(ARG)

(USSR)

(ARG)

(UK)

(ARG)

(USSR)

(ARG)

(USA)

(UK)

(UK)

(USSR)

(AUST)

(USA)

(USA)

(USSR)

(USSR)

(USA)

(USSR)

(USSR)

(USSR)

(USSR)

(AUST)

(USA)

(NZ)

(USA)

(FR)

(USA)(NZ)

(SOV)

Permanent bases ■

Seasonal bases ☐

Air routes —

Un-exploited

Iron ♦

Other ores ●

Copper ▲

Uranium ★

Coal ▨

Drake

Strait

South Pacific

BOUNTY

AUCKLAND I.

## Antarctica

Since 1900, seven states have claimed territorial rights over portions of the Antarctic continent:

United Kingdom (1908)
New Zealand (1923)
France (1924 and 1938)
Australia (1933)
Norway (1939)
Chile (1940)
Argentina (1943)

More recently, Brazil has added itself to this list.

This partition is largely formal, since the United States, the USSR, and other states have always reserved their claims.

Brazil, Chile, and Argentina base their claims on geographic proximity, the latter two disputing rights asserted by the British. The British, by maintaining their sovereignty over the Falkland Islands in 1982, continue to exercise de facto authority over the sector they laid claim to in 1908.

On Antarctica itself, several countries have an effective presence, permanent or seasonal, in the form of meteorological or scientific stations: in quantitative order, the USSR (12), the USA (9), Argentina (8), Australia (3), Japan (2), New Zealand (3), United Kingdom (4), France (1).

## The Falkland Islands and Antarctica

73

# The World from Antarctica

## Depth of Main Transit Routes (meters)

CALAIS (31)
GIBRALTAR (+ 100)
SUEZ (14.5)
BAB EL MANDAB (+ 100)
HORMUZ (+ 60)
PANAMA (11.9)
MALACCA (18)
SUNDA (30)
TORRES STRAIT (10)
TASMANIA (+ 50)

## Main Sea Routes and Principal Strategic Waterways

The importance of sea power in history no longer requires demonstration, but it is a factor that is all too often overlooked by those who have regional—that is provincial—perspectives. It was sea power that ensured Anglo-American supremacy. In spite of the development of Soviet naval power over the last two decades, key strategic points are controlled by the United States and its allies. Their security is absolutely vital for the maritime trade of the Western powers.

- USSR and allies
- USA and allies
- ★ Strategic points
- Major sea lanes

TASMANIA
STRAIT OF LOMBOK
STRAIT OF SUNDA
STRAIT OF MALACCA
KOREA STRAIT
FORMOSA STRAIT
SRI LANKA
STRAIT OF HORMUZ
BAB EL MANDEB
SOMALIA
NORTH SEA
DENMARK STRAIT
FAEROE IS.
ENGLISH CHANNEL
GIBRALTAR
FLORIDA STRAIT
MONA PASSAGE
PANAMA
STRAIT OF MOZAMBIQUE
CAPE VERDE
CAPE OF GOOD HOPE
CAPE HORN

# SECURITY PERCEPTIONS OF THE UNITED STATES, THE USSR, AND REGIONAL AND MIDDLE POWERS

# How the United States Was Settled

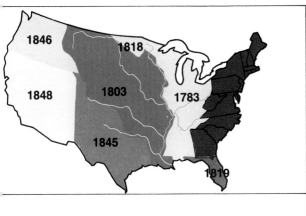

Occupied in 1800
Occupied about 1850
Occupied about 1900

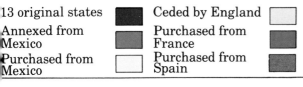

13 original states
Annexed from Mexico
Purchased from Mexico
Ceded by England
Purchased from France
Purchased from Spain

**Territorial Growth**

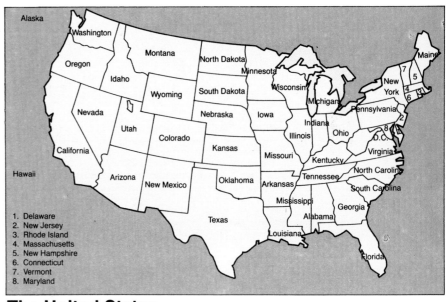

1. Delaware
2. New Jersey
3. Rhode Island
4. Massachusetts
5. New Hampshire
6. Connecticut
7. Vermont
8. Maryland

**The United States**

# The United States:
# Formation and Settlement

In the first phase of its expansion, the United States was able, without fighting any major wars, rapidly to occupy its hinterland. It had no rivals on the continent. It was soon making its presence felt outside the continent (Liberia, 1820; Japan, 1854; China, 1859), and by the turn of the century had ensured its economic dominance over the American continent and occupied the Pacific as far as the Philippines. Until the Korean war, the USA had known only absolute victories, total successes: the conquest of the West, the purchase of land from foreign powers (Alaska in 1867), wars against Mexico and Spain. The interventions in 1917 and 1941 themselves were wars in which the United States was protected by its geographic isolation.

As a business society with an empirical philosophy, a Protestant ethic, and a liberal democracy with great social mobility, the United States, proud of having neither colonies nor rivals, had not throughout its history developed any real conception of interstate relations. Not having known the realities that spring from a constant struggle for national self-preservation, the United States became a world power with a historical experience very different from that of the European states.

After World War II, the United States, the dominant state on the planet, found itself faced with the task of containing Communist expansion (1947).

Strong in its nuclear monopoly, then enjoying an undeniable superiority for two decades, the United States sought first and foremost to contain this expansion systematically.

The American withdrawal, noticeable after the war in Vietnam (1973), which profoundly affected public opinion, and consequently American political will, is to be traced to a number of factors: conceptual weakness* and lack of knowledge of the outside world; frequent confusion of national aspirations with the expansion of communism; defense of notoriously corrupt and ineffective allies solely because they are pliable, combined with an inability to support allies that have been promised security. As for decisions, they are generally made in moments of crisis, while long-term planning is neglected.

However, by reintroducing human rights as a political point of reference, the United States launched the first Western ideological counteroffensive in four decades, not to mention, more recently, an ambitious rearmament program intended to reassert its superiority.

Whatever its economic difficulties, the United States possesses the necessary technological advances, the resources, and the dynamism to continue to be the leading power in the world.

*The Nixon–Kissinger team is an exception.

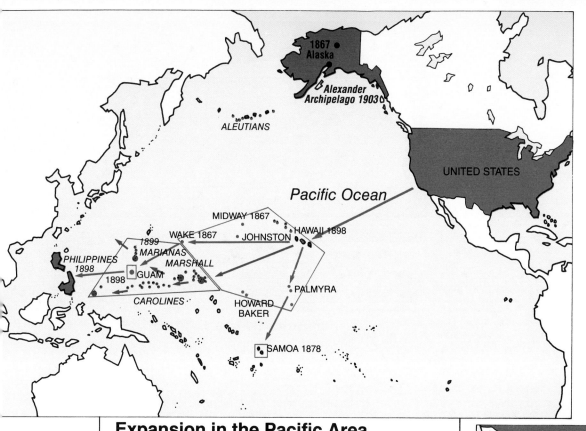

# Expansion in the Pacific

1945—Micronesia
(Marianas, Carolines,
Marshalls,
Western Samoa)

The Philippines,
an American colony
since 1898,
became independent
in 1945.

**1867 Alaska**

*Alexander Archipelago 1903*

ALEUTIANS

UNITED STATES

*Pacific Ocean*

MIDWAY 1867

WAKE 1867  JOHNSTON  HAWAII 1898

*1899*
*MARIANAS*
*MARSHALL*

PHILIPPINES
1898

1898  GUAM

CAROLINES

HOWARD
BAKER

PALMYRA

SAMOA 1878

## Expansion in the Pacific Area

In 1945      In the 19th century

## The United States in Central America

## Interventions in the Caribbean Basin

There have been some fifteen major
interventions in
the Caribbean basin
between 1903 (Panama)
and 1965 (Dominican
Republic)

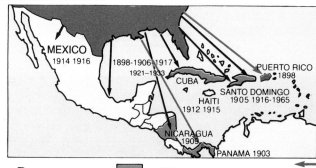

MEXICO
1914 1916

1898-1906 1917
1921–1933

CUBA

PUERTO RICO
1898

SANTO DOMINGO
1905 1916-1965

HAITI
1912 1915

NICARAGUA
1909

PANAMA 1903

Protectorates    US interventions

Other countries  USA and annexations

## Minorities in the United States

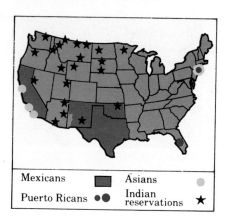

| Mexicans | ◼ | Asians | ⬤ |
| Puerto Ricans | ⬤⬤ | Indian reservations | ★ |

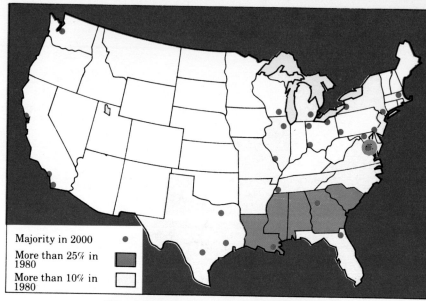

| Majority in 2000 | ⬤ |
| More than 25% in 1980 | ◼ |
| More than 10% in 1980 | ☐ |

### Blacks in the United States

While the Indian minority forms only a tiny percentage of the population, blacks and Hispanics (such as the Chicanos or the Puerto Ricans) number some 50 million individuals: blacks, 26.5 million; Hispanics, 14.5 million (1980). In addition there are 8 million illegal aliens.

With Asians* and other minorities, the United States population is 20 to 22 percent "nonwhite." Blacks, increasingly numerous in the metropolitan areas of the Northeast and the West (New York, Philadelphia, Washington, Detroit, Chicago, Los Angeles, San Diego, Seattle), are also concentrated in several cities in the South (Houston, Dallas, Memphis, Atlanta). Hispanics are mainly settled in California, New Mexico, and Texas, and in the following cities: Los Angeles, New York, El Paso, Miami, San Antonio.

It is estimated that, since 1975, legally or otherwise, about 1 million immigrants have entered the United States each year, 82 percent of them from Latin America or Asia. Over the last decade, Los Angeles has come to play the role formerly held by New York as the mecca for immigrants from all over the world. The combination of poverty and racial tensions, particularly among blacks, intensifies the feeling of insecurity in the big cities.

---

*The Asian communities (Japanese, Chinese, Koreans, and so on) are often well-to-do.

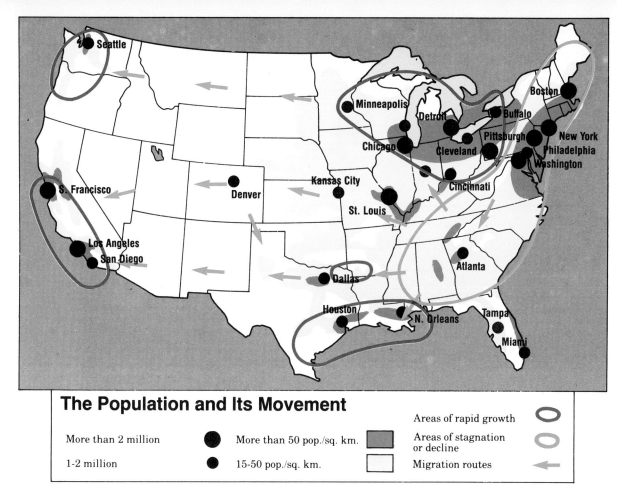

## The Population and Its Movement

More than 2 million ●

1-2 million ●

More than 50 pop./sq. km. ■

15-50 pop./sq. km. ●

Areas of rapid growth ⬭

Areas of stagnation or decline ⬭

Migration routes ←

# United States: Internal Migrations

The old industrial East, bordered by the Great Lakes–Washington–Boston triangle, is increasingly being replaced, in terms of resources and soon in terms of population, by the West, especially California and Texas.

Migration movements, both internal and external (coming mainly from Mexico and the Caribbean), are toward the southern and western parts of the country. A gradual movement of the country's center of gravity is thus under way.

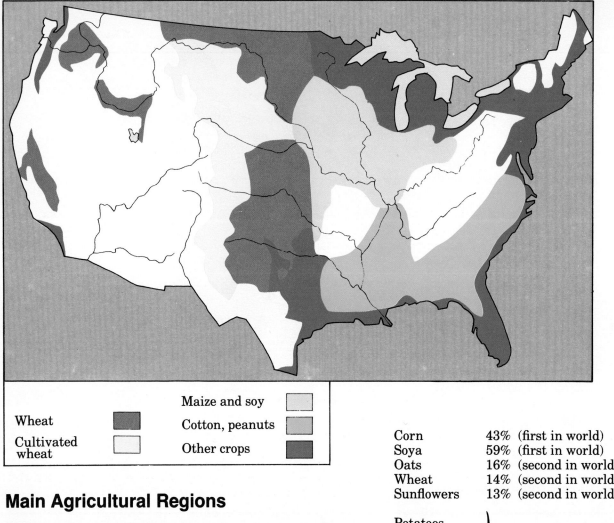

| | | |
|---|---|---|
| Wheat | | |
| Cultivated wheat | | |
| Maize and soy | | |
| Cotton, peanuts | | |
| Other crops | | |

## Main Agricultural Regions

Thanks to a remarkable productivity, the United States is the leading agricultural producer in the world. It is far and away the leading exporter of grains and soya products.

| | | |
|---|---|---|
| Corn | 43% | (first in world) |
| Soya | 59% | (first in world) |
| Oats | 16% | (second in world) |
| Wheat | 14% | (second in world) |
| Sunflowers | 13% | (second in world) |

Potatoes
Sugar beets
Peanuts          } (third in world)
Beef
Pork

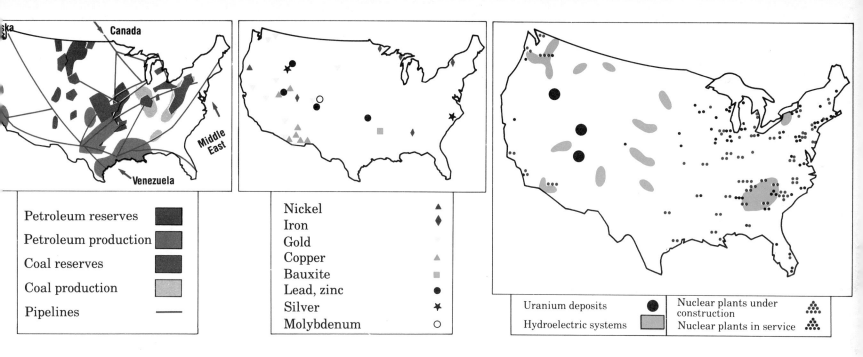

**Legend (left map):**
- Petroleum reserves
- Petroleum production
- Coal reserves
- Coal production
- Pipelines

**Legend (middle map):**
- Nickel ▲
- Iron ◆
- Gold
- Copper ▲
- Bauxite ■
- Lead, zinc ●
- Silver ✶
- Molybdenum ○

**Legend (right map):**
- Uranium deposits ●
- Hydroelectric systems ▬
- Nuclear plants under construction
- Nuclear plants in service

# United States: Resources

With substantial energy and mineral resources, the United States remains the world's leading industrial power.

In leading sectors such as aerospace, aeronautics, computers, and nuclear development, the United States effectively demonstrates its determination to maintain or increase its lead.

**Minerals**

| | | |
|---|---|---|
| Copper | 15% | (first in world) |
| Iron | 8% | (third in world) |
| Lead | 15% | (second in world) |
| Zinc | 6% | (fifth in world) |
| Silver | 10% | (fourth in world) |

Gold, nickel, bauxite, etc.

**Energy Resources**

| | | |
|---|---|---|
| Coal | 25% | (first in world) |
| Uranium | 36% | (first in world) |
| Natural gas | 35% | (first in world) |
| Petroleum | 15% | (third in world) |
| Hydroelectricity | | (first in world) |

# Industrial Centers

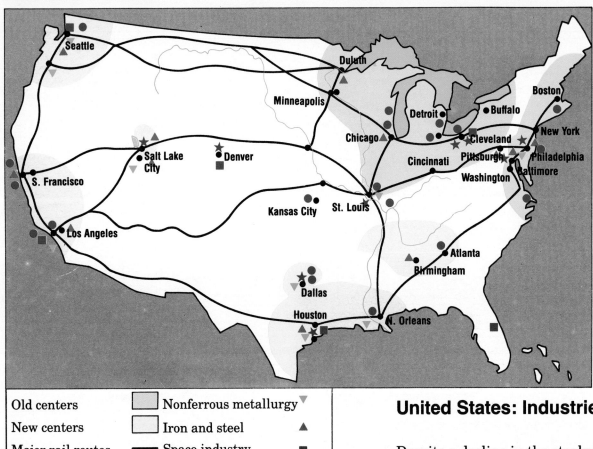

Old centers  
New centers  
Major rail routes  
Chemical industries ★  

Nonferrous metallurgy ▼  
Iron and steel ▲  
Space industry ■  
Autos, ships, planes ●  

Information industry: the Northeast, Texas

**Map labels:** Seattle, Duluth, Minneapolis, Detroit, Buffalo, Boston, Chicago, Cleveland, New York, Cincinnati, Pittsburgh, Philadelphia, Baltimore, Washington, Salt Lake City, Denver, S. Francisco, Kansas City, St. Louis, Los Angeles, Atlanta, Birmingham, Dallas, Houston, N. Orleans

# United States: Industries

Despite a decline in the steelmaking and engineering industries, the Northeast still remains the traditional stronghold of heavy industry.

The South (particularly Texas), the Pacific coast, and more recently the Rockies (around Salt Lake City and Denver) are undergoing rapid development thanks to new industrial sectors (nuclear energy, aeronautics, chemistry).

# Canada: A Federal State

## Agricultural Regions

| | |
|---|---|
| French-speaking Quebec | |
| Forests | |
| Various crops | |
| Grain regions | |

## A Rich Subsoil

| | |
|---|---|
| Petroleum | |
| Pipelines | |
| Coal | |
| Iron | |
| Uranium | |
| Copper | |
| Silver | |
| Gold | |
| Hydroelectricity | |

## A RESERVOIR OF RESOURCES

Situated between the United States and Alaska, Canada is marked by its vast size, its continental climate with an exceptionally harsh winter, and its very small population. Settlement quite closely follows the line of the border with the United States, although the country also has an Arctic inclination. The economy is largely integrated into the United States market.

Does such a situation encourage the building of a nation? Paradoxically, the particularism of French-speaking Quebec, involving a degree of linguistic and cultural opposition to the United States and Anglo-American hegemony, may contribute to nationhood.

### Energy and Mineral Resources

| | | |
|---|---|---|
| Petroleum | 3% | (w.p.) res.* |
| Gas | 4.5 | (w.p.) res. |
| Uranium | 16 | (w.p.) res. 19% |
| Hydroelectricity | 16 | (w.p.) |
| Iron | 5.5 | (w.p.) res. 8.5% |

*(w.p.) res. = (world production) reserves.

# USSR: Historical Expansion

About 1450

1500-1750

1790-1914

Long occupied by the Mongols (thirteenth through fifteenth centuries), Russia has undergone two processes: The first, uninterrupted since the sixteenth century, was the conquest of its hinterland, followed by imperial conquests at the expense particularly of the Ottoman and Chinese empires; the other was the pursuit of Europeanization to overcome its backwardness.

If we ignore Leninism and socialist ideology, we see that the Soviet Union has retained and increased the imperial heritage in new forms. Since the beginning of the five-year plans, it has been attempting to make up for its industrial backwardness and to develop its military capacities.

In 1948 Finland and Yugoslavia left the Soviet sphere of influence.

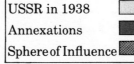

| | |
|---|---|
| USSR in 1938 | |
| Annexations | |
| Sphere of Influence | |

# The Conquest of the East

Stages in the
occupation of the land

| Before 1920 | |
| 1920-1955 | |
| After 1955 | |
| Railways | |

## USSR

Although tsarist Russia conquered Siberia over the last few centuries and built the first Trans-Siberian railway, significant settlement, the development of communications, and industrialization date from the last five decades. Southern Siberia has been settled mostly by Slavs. In this way, despite ideological rivalries, Europe has reached the Pacific. American conquest of its Far West corresponds, making all due allowances, to the Russian conquest of the East.

## Expansion of the Slavs in the USSR

**Industrial Expansion Eastward**

## Soviet Strategic Bases

### USSR

The nuclear sites stretch through Soviet territory along a line that closely follows the area of Slav settlement.

Kazakhstan, which is the only Muslim republic to have major nuclear and aerospace sites, has a population that is 43 percent Slav.

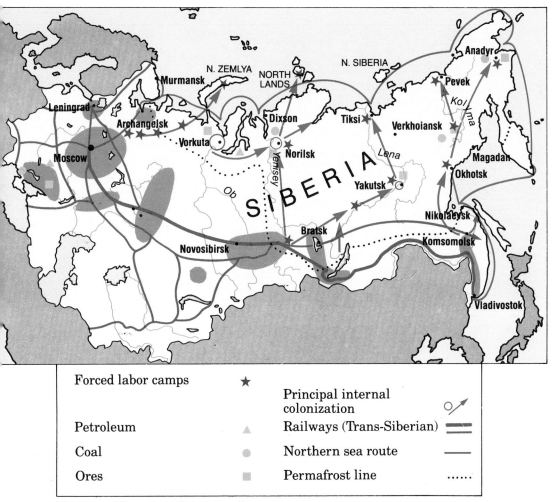

## USSR

Moving out from the Trans-Siberian railway, the gradual and arduous conquest of northern Siberia has been carried out along the great rivers (Ob, Yenisey, Lena, Kolyma), and along the main sea route linking the White Sea and Vladivostok through the Arctic Ocean. The Soviets use icebreakers that have no equal in the world. It is likely that the Siberian camps have played a not insignificant part in the process of opening up the area.

| | | | |
|---|---|---|---|
| Forced labor camps | ★ | Principal internal colonization | o/↗ |
| Petroleum | ▲ | Railways (Trans-Siberian) | ═══ |
| Coal | ● | Northern sea route | ── |
| Ores | ■ | Permafrost line | ...... |

## Expansion to the Far North

Railways
Peoples of the Caucasus
Muslims of Central Asia
Emirate of Bokhara

## Sovietization of the Peoples of the Caucasus and the Muslim Peoples of Central Asia

In these regions, some groups have been given autonomous status: Cherkesses (1922), Abkhazes (1921), Ossetes (1924), Ingouches (1934), Kara Kalpaks (1925), Ouigours, Adjars, and so on.

# USSR

Muslim Central Asia and the Islamic part of the Caucasus were conquered during the nineteenth century, often in the face of fierce resistance.

Today these regions are divided into six republics. This division was established by the Bolshevik government at Stalin's instigation. The Emirate of Bokhara was annexed and divided among several republics in 1920 and was the scene of a prolonged uprising (1920–1928). The nationalities policy seeks to differentiate rather than to unify ethnic groups that are relatively homogeneous (only the Tadjiks are not Turkish-speaking).

The alphabet adopted for the transcription of the languages of these republics is Cyrillic (1928). The population growth rate is distinctly higher than that of the Slav groups. The economic growth of these republics has been spectacular, and Uzbekistan has long been held up as a model for the countries of the Middle East. Georgia and Armenia were sovietized in 1920, after a short-lived independence. These two republics are not Muslim.

# The USSR: A Multinational State
## The Fifteen Republics and the Principal Autonomous Republics

**Legend:**
- Frontiers of federal republics ——
- Frontiers, autonomous republics ——
- Slavic republics �as shaded
- Muslim republics ▢
- Caucasian republics ▢
- Other republics ▢

Map labels: ESTONIA, KARELIA, LITHUANIA, LATVIA, BYELORUSSIA, Moscow, KOMI, YAKOUTI, MOLDAVIA, UKRAINE, MORDOVIA, R S F S R, MARI, UDMURT, CHUVASH, TATAR, BASHKIR, RUSSIA, ABKHAZ, GEORGIA, KALMYK, DAGESTAN, ARMENIA, AZERBAIJAN, KAZAKHSTAN, KARA-KALPAK, GORNO ALTAI, BURYAT, TUVINIA, UZBEKISTAN, TURKMENISTAN, KIRGHIZ, TADJIKISTAN

In terms of area, the Soviet Union is the largest country in the world (22,000,000 sq. km.), but most of its population lives in the west and south, 70 percent of the population living in the European part on 20 percent of its area. Siberia holds great strategic interest; in addition to its area, it contains vast mineral and forest resources potentially exploitable or already being exploited. But there are only 25 million inhabitants in its 13,000,000 sq. km. On its eastern flank, the USSR controls the Sea of Okhotsk.

While one Soviet citizen in two is not Russian, the other nationalities (officially there are 126 of them) are an extremely diverse group. The two most numerous groups are the Slavs (Ukrainians and Byelorussians)—some 50 million—and the Muslims, mostly Turkish-speaking, who number almost 50 million but who are divided among six republics.

The government of this bureaucratic and totalitarian society rests on the organization provided by the single party, the guarantor of ideological orthodoxy; by the KGB, the guarantor of security; and by the army, the guarantor of Soviet power in the world. The system contains a series of contradictions: agriculture/industry; heavy industry/consumer goods; military sector/civilian sector (marked by bottlenecks, waste, and corruption); national, religious, and political problems. This system, in the framework of its contradictions, engenders passivity, black markets (which often act as regulators), and low productivity.

However, strategically the system benefits from the advantages of its militarized structure, from its secretiveness, from its political cohesion (once goals have been laid down), from the control of its public opinion, and from the role still played by its ideology within and beyond its frontiers. These advantages amply compensate for the ponderous bureaucracy and mitigate the relative lack of dynamism and the shortcomings of the economic machinery.

The USSR is the world's second economic power, just ahead of Japan, and its power is above all military. This military power has been considerably developed and modernized over the last two decades. In a context where the United States was politically paralyzed by the outcome of the Vietnam war, the Soviet Union exploited the vacuums in Angola, Ethiopia, and Afghanistan and demonstrated its logistical capabilities.

## The Subsoil of the Soviet Union

### ENERGY RESOURCE

Oil and natural gas
Coal
Hydroelectricity
Uranium
Nuclear energy

### METALS

Platinum
Silver
Chrome
Manganese
Nickel
Lead-Zinc-Tin
Iron
Copper
Gold
Bauxite

70% in Europe on 20% of the territory
30% in Asia on 80% of the territory
126 nationalities, but 15 republics*

| | |
|---|---|
| Russia | 137 million (83% Russian) |
| The Ukraine | 50 million (20% Russian) |
| Uzbekistan | 15 million (12.5% Russian) |
| Kazakhstan | 14.5 million (43% Russian) |
| Byelorussia | 9.5 million (10.5% Russian) |
| Azerbaijan | 5.9 million (10% Russian) |
| Georgia | 5 million (8.5% Russian) |
| Moldavia | 4 million (12% Russian) |
| Tadjikistan | 3.7 million (12% Russian) |
| Kirghiz Republic | 3.5 million (30% Russian) |
| Lithuania | 3.4 million (8.5% Russian) |
| Armenia | 3 million (2.7% Russian) |
| Turkmenistan | 2.7 million (15% Russian) |
| Latvia | 2.5 million (30% Russian) |
| Estonia | 1.5 million (25% Russian) |

*126 nationalities are officially recognized. The fifteen with more than a million inhabitants form the Federated Socialist Soviet Republics. Depending on their size (in terms of population), the others form autonomous republics or autonomous territories (notably the nomadic peoples).

The Soviets have linked up their various operational theaters by means of a network of canals connecting five seas: the Sea of Azov, the Black Sea, the Caspian Sea, the Baltic Sea, and the White Sea. Ships under 5,000 tons can use them.

| | |
|---|---|
| Navigable waterways | |
| Canals | |
| Dams | |

**The North–South Waterway Link**

## USSR/Middle East

The maps show Soviet aspirations in the region that they had hoped to control through the Nazi–Soviet Pact (1939).

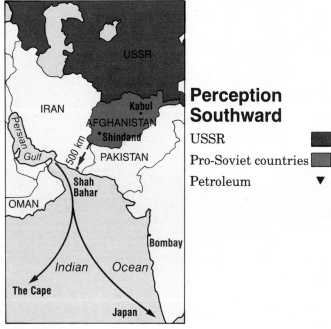

### Perception Southward

USSR ▮

Pro-Soviet countries ▮

Petroleum ▼

## Afghanistan

The Soviet intervention in Afghanistan (December 1979) brought the Soviets to within 500 km. of the Indian Ocean and underlined the vulnerability of a Pakistan already weakened by its Indian rival.

Coming on top of the fall of the Shah of Iran, this intervention reduced virtually to nil the American position in the Near East.

**Asia Seen from Moscow**

AUSTRALIA

INDONESIA

*Pacific Ocean*

SINGAPORE

PHILIPPINES

MALAYSIA

*Indian Ocean*

VIETNAM

THAILAND

SRI LANKA

TAIWAN

BURMA

BANGLADESH

S. KOREA

CHINA

INDIA

N. KOREA

PAKISTAN

JAPAN

AFGHANISTAN

OMAN

S. YEMEN

MONGOLIA

IRAN

SAUDI ARABIA

IRAQ

USSR

SYRIA

ISRAEL

Moscow

TURKEY

LEBANON

For the USSR, whose northern reaches are in the polar region and which has limited access to the open sea, it is vital to have maritime staging areas for its rapidly growing fleet along the peninsular and insular belt of Asia. Geopolitical logic would require the Soviet Union to have control of the arc running from the Indian subcontinent to the Horn of Africa.

## Perception Northward

Beyond the Arctic lies
the hostile world
of North America.

# Europe: Two Blocks of Hostile States

Western Europe, the center of the planet until 1918 and the continent on which was played out the future of the world until 1945, is marked today by its political division, its economic power, and its relative military vulnerability.

Whereas the whole of Central Europe fell into the Soviet orbit in 1945, Western Europe, with American support, was able to maintain its overall position. Austria and Finland retained or regained their independence through their neutrality. The only retreats in the Soviet camp, in Yugoslavia (1948) and Albania (1960), were due not to Western pressure, but to the contradictions engendered by Soviet hegemony, and were made possible by the nationalism and determination of the Yugoslav and Albanian leaders.

The Helsinki Accords (1976) gave the official stamp to the de facto partition of the European continent.

| Legend | |
|---|---|
| Iron Curtain | |
| USSR | |
| Warsaw Pact | |
| Other Socialist countries | |
| Neutral states | |
| NATO nations | |
| Western allies | |

The USSR has retained control of its shield in Eastern Europe, despite some violent crises (Berlin, 1953; Budapest, 1956; Czechoslovakia, 1968; Poland, 1980–1982).

Begun by the Marshall Plan, the recovery of Western Europe, which between 1945 and 1973 benefited from very favorable world economic conditions, was consolidated around the European Economic Community (the EEC), to which ten countries have gradually adhered. Despite various proposals, the EEC has led neither to political integration nor to the elaboration of a strictly European common defense within the Atlantic Alliance.

Western Europe, as it is defined in the framework of the EEC—and consequently the middle powers that belong to it—seems to have regional interests articulated around Eurafrica and the Mediterranean basin. West Germany, the leading economic power in Western Europe, remains politically determined by its past, the division of the German nation, and its geographical situation to the east.

For Germany as for France, the Franco-German alliance represents the heart of Europe. For many years France was bogged down in Indochina and Algeria in rearguard wars. After leaving NATO, while remaining a member of the Atlantic Alliance, France acquired nuclear firepower and laid down a strategy of self-protection based on deterrence of the strong by the weak. It is France that, politically and diplomatically, has conceptualized and continues to guarantee the Eurafrican—and Mediterranean—strategy for Europe, guided by a foreign policy laid down by General de Gaulle.

In spite of a distinct decline, the only other nuclear power, the United Kingdom—a latecomer into the Common Market—continues to retain a not insignificant weight in a number of sectors (finance, nuclear power, shipping, oil).

Great Britain, the creator of the first worldwide colonial empire, which laid the basis of the contemporary preeminence of the English language, has also been responsible for a large share of postcolonial conflicts and crises: the Indian subcontinent, the Israeli–Arab conflict, Cyprus, and so on. Great Britain has gradually abandoned most of the strategic positions it held, including the Persian Gulf region, to the benefit of the United States (1971). The Falklands war (1982) demonstrated the political determination of an old European power, its logistical capability, and the high quality of its professional army.

Italy, the fourth great European power, has vigorously industrialized over the last three decades. But the problem of the backwardness of its Mezzogiorno remains unchanged.

In the north, bordering neutral Finland and Sweden, NATO member Norway has a vulnerable Arctic position opposite one of the key zones of the Soviet military system.

The current debate concerning the Soviet SS-20s and the possible installation of American Pershings in the European theater so as to reestablish a credible deterrent touches directly on the balance on which the peace is based.

Gibraltar is the only interstate problem (United Kingdom–Spain) remaining in Europe.

# Europe and the East

**Economic and Military Presence of the United States**

1000 US companies ●    + 100 US companies ●
500 US companies ●    − 100 US companies ·
250 US companies ●    Military bases ★

EEC
Other Western nations
USSR and allies

SS 20 (range 4300 km)

URALS

Moscow

Berlin

Soviet military power is felt as a threat to Western Europe.

**Population Density**

More than 100 pop./sq. km. ▉
50-100 pop./sq. km. ▒
Fewer than 50 pop./sq. km. ☐

Rich Europe ▒
Middle income ▒
Poor Europe ☐

**Rich Europe, Poor Europe**

More than 8% of pop. ▉
6-8% of pop. ▒
Less than 6% of pop. ▒
Countries of emigration ☐

Black Africa →
Asia and the West Indies →
Islamic countries →
Europe →

Immigration zone ▬

**Immigrants in Western Europe**

Western Europe is particularly heavily populated and, like all industrialized areas, has a very low population growth rate.

The EEC includes the most prosperous states (except for neutral countries such as Sweden and Switzerland, a financial center of the highest importance).

Europe, like the United States and the Persian Gulf countries, is a magnet for migrant workers (about 11 million). The percentage of migrants hovers around 7.5 for France, West Germany, the United Kingdom, and Belgium; 6 percent for Austria; 5 percent for Sweden; 4 percent for the Netherlands; 1.5 percent for Denmark; 17 percent for Switzerland; and over 30 percent for Luxembourg.

A source of hard currency for their home countries, the immigrant workers constitute a pool of cheap labor for the host countries; they pose a special political problem in times of economic crisis for the host countries and a source of dislocation in the event of massive repatriation to their homelands.

**THE BASQUE PEOPLE**

**LINGUISTIC CONFLICT IN BELGIUM**

Flemish
Walloon
Bilingual

German speaking
German Walloon
Flemish Walloon

**THE IRISH QUESTION**

Catholic
10 to 30%     50 to 80%
30 to 50%     80% plus

# Minority Problems

Caught between the idea of the nation-state and the idea of human rights, both born of the Enlightenment, and both of which mark the emergence of individual rights as well as modern nationalism, the rights of minorities (particularly ethnic ones) have been largely neglected. It is often a crucial problem in Third World countries, but minorities in Europe, including those in the liberal democratic countries, have suffered or still suffer more or less overt oppression or pressure for assimilation. In Central Europe: Hungarians in Transylvania (Romania); Albanians in Yugoslavia; and so on. In Western Europe: Irish Catholics in Ulster; Catalans and Basques in Spain; and, in a more specific way, the Flemish-Walloon conflict (originating in Walloon predominance until recently) in Belgium.

These more or less conflict-laden situations, often the result of pressures toward centralism, are generally resolved by either autonomy or federalism.

Unlike ethnic difficulties elsewhere, in Western Europe minorities are internal problems that do not precipitate destabilizing interference from other states.

# Main Agricultural Regions in the EEC

Unlike its European neighbors, France is one of the leading world exporters of grain. Europe's livestock industry is important. Agribusiness is developing rapidly and, in a world context, agriculture remains one of Europe's best assets.

**Significance of the EEC in the World**

| (Percent of World Production) | |
|---|---|
| Wheat | 12% |
| Barley | 22 |
| Sugar | 14 |
| Milk | 26 |
| Meat | 15 |
| Corn | 4 |

*Note: Spain and Portugal have applied to join the EEC.*

Cereals (EEC)

Cereals (Spain, Portugal)

Livestock (EEC)

Livestock (Spain, Portugal)

# Europe: Industrial Power

The EEC is the world's second greatest industrial power—the leading one in terms of manufacturing output—just behind the United States.

Of the ten nations, West Germany alone produces almost half of most of the industrial goods produced by Europe.

Since the end of World War II, Europe's weakness in energy and mineral resources has continued to grow and constitutes—as it does for Japan, but to a lesser extent—a serious handicap.

### EEC (% of world total)

#### Energy

| | |
|---|---|
| Coal | 11% |
| Hydroelectricity | 16% |
| Nuclear power | 20% |
| Oil | 0.75% |
| Ores | slight |

#### Output

| | |
|---|---|
| Steel | 18% |
| Aluminum | 13% |
| Automobile manufacture | 33% |
| Industrial equipment | 13% |
| Shipbuilding | 20% |
| Synthetic rubber | 21% |
| Synthetic fibers | 20% |

| | |
|---|---|
| Industrial areas | |
| Principal centers | |
| Underdeveloped areas | |

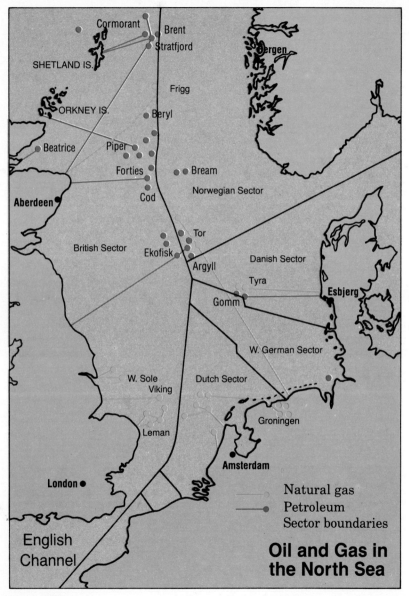

**Oil and Gas in the North Sea**

Cormorant
Brent
Stratfjord
SHETLAND IS.
Bergen
Frigg
Beryl
ORKNEY IS.
Piper
Beatrice
Forties
Bream
Cod
Norwegian Sector
Aberdeen
British Sector
Tor
Ekofisk
Argyll
Danish Sector
Tyra
Esbjerg
Gomm
W. German Sector
W. Sole
Viking
Dutch Sector
Groningen
Leman
Amsterdam
London
English Channel

Natural gas
Petroleum
Sector boundaries

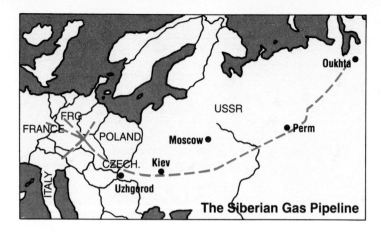

**The Siberian Gas Pipeline**

Oukhta
FRG
FRANCE
POLAND
USSR
Moscow
Perm
ITALY
CZECH.
Kiev
Uzhgorod

## Western Europe and Its Energy Needs

To facilitate economic exchanges and to show its independence, the EEC has made a number of trade agreements:
- 1977—industrial free trade with the states of the former Free Trade Area (Switzerland, Austria, Sweden)
- 1978—periodic agreement with non-European states in the framework of GATT
- 1978—Lomé Convention, with a number of African, Caribbean, and Pacific and Indian Ocean states
- Various bilateral agreements (Yugoslavia, Romania)
- Agreements with Spain, Portugal, and Turkey, all candidates for admission to the EEC (Greece has been a member since 1980.)

USSR and allies

ICELAND · MOROCCO · TUNISIA · SYRIA · ISRAEL · IRAQ · IRAN · AFGHANISTAN · JORDAN · ALGERIA · LIBYA · EGYPT · SAUDI ARABIA · OMAN · UNITED ARAB EMIRATES · CAPE VERDE · MAURITANIA · MALI · NIGER · CHAD · SUDAN · YEMEN · S. YEMEN · DJIBOUTI · SENEGAL · GAMBIA · GUINEA BISSAU · GUINEA · UPPER VOLTA · BENIN · NIGERIA · CAMEROON · CENTRAL AFRICAN REP. · ETHIOPIA · SIERRA LEONE · IVORY COAST · GHANA · TOGO · LIBERIA · S. TOMÉ · EQUAT. GUINEA · GABON · CONGO · UGANDA · KENYA · SOMALIA · RWANDA · BURUNDI · ZAIRE · TANZANIA · COMOROS · ANGOLA · MALAWI · ZAMBIA · MOZAMBIQUE · MADAGASCAR · MAURITIUS · RÉUNION · NAMIBIA · ZIMBABWE · BOTSWANA · SOUTH AFRICA · SWAZILAND · LESOTHO

Atlantic Ocean

Indian Ocean

EEC
Lomé Convention
Other Western nations
Arab-Islamic world
USSR and allies
Petroleum routes

# Geopolitical and Geostrategic Aspects of Western Europe

The regional geostrategic area of Western Europe includes Africa, the Mediterranean basin, and the Persian Gulf, which determines policy toward the Arab states. By signing the Lomé Convention (1979) with 43 African states, the EEC created a system for regulating economic relations and thus made it possible to hope for relative stability in its traditional area of activity in Africa. Several small states in the Caribbean and the Pacific were also signatories to this convention.

### The Organization of African Unity (OAU)
Founded 1963. Includes all the African states, as well as the Saharan Arab Democratic Republic and the islands of Cape Verde, São Tomé and Principe, Mauritius, the Comoros, and the Seychelles—except Namibia and South Africa. The problem of recognition of the Saharan Arab Democratic Republic, supported by Algeria and opposed by Morocco, divides the OAU.

# Africa

Sub-Saharan Africa had remained largely outside East–West confrontations until 1975, but since the withdrawal of Portugal and the radicalization of Ethiopia (1977), it has ceased to be a Western preserve. Until that date, the major strategic issues in the Third World had been fought out along the peninsular belt that stretches from the eastern Mediterranean to the Far East. The USSR had made its presence felt in Egypt, Guinea, Zaire, Sudan, and Somalia, though generally without much success: withdrawal from Egypt, failure in Zaire, cool relations with Guinea, withdrawal from Sudan, expulsion from Somalia. The end of Portuguese colonialism created a vacuum that the USSR boldly exploited in concert with Cuba, and that created a new situation militarily, in both Angola and Ethiopia.

Although what is at stake in Africa is not vital, either for the United States or for the Soviet Union—although it is for Europe—southern Africa has an important role to play in terms of access to raw materials essential to the West and to Japan. South Africa is the only regional power there.

At the end of two decades of independence, the balance sheet in terms of development in sub-Saharan Africa is meager. The conditions typical of most African states are decline or stagnation of agriculture, and economic stagnation for the vast majority that lack a raw materials export base.

Contrary to the desires of the Organization of African Unity, all the inter-African associations launched over the last twenty years have collapsed. Even the principle of the inviolability of frontiers, which had been respected over quite a long period, has been broken over the last few years by sovereign states: the Somali-Ethiopian war over the Ogaden; annexation by Libya of a strip of land 100,000 kilometers square in northern Chad.

With an average rate of population increase of over 2.5 percent, projections give the following growth: 220 million in 1950, 350 million in 1970, and over 800 million in 2000.

To handicaps of recent origin, such as Balkanization, monoculture, economies geared to serve outside needs, and heavy cultural dependence, must be added others with deeper roots: ethnic divisions and antagonisms; low levels of social stratification, and low levels of productive forces.

Africa south of the Sahara is marked by weak states and virtually nonexistent nations.

It seems unlikely that there will be any major changes in the short term in the continuation of Western, and particularly European, influence in Africa. But unlike the Soviet assistance that turned sour in Egypt and Somalia, the Cuban military presence guarantees the survival of a Soviet presence insofar as it ensures the survival of existing regimes. This is particularly true in Angola.

With a Eurafrican geopolitical perspective, the EEC signed the important Lomé Convention (1979) and set up a stabilization system for export receipts for basic products, accepted the duty-free entry of most products exported by its African associated states, and substantially increased its annual assistance ($4 billion).

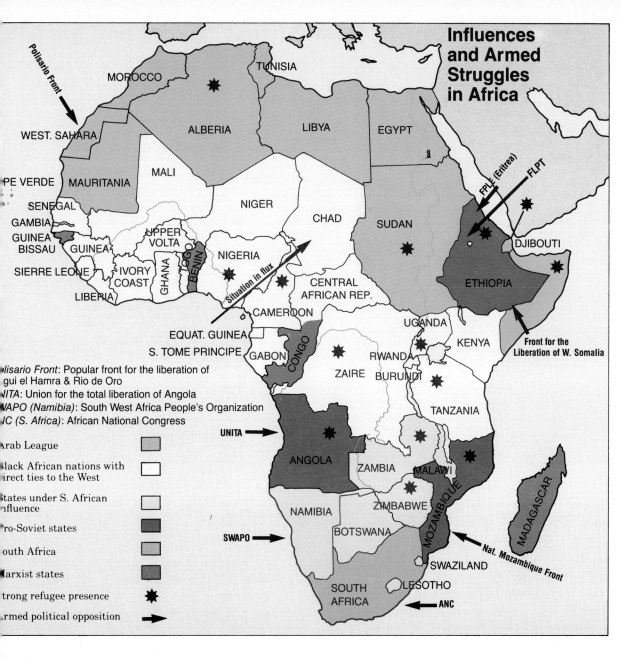

## Influences and Armed Struggles in Africa

Polisario Front

MOROCCO
TUNISIA
WEST. SAHARA
ALBERIA
LIBYA
EGYPT
PE VERDE
MAURITANIA
MALI
SENEGAL
NIGER
GAMBIA
CHAD
SUDAN
GUINEA BISSAU
UPPER VOLTA
GUINEA
NIGERIA
SIERRE LEONE
IVORY COAST
GHANA
TOGO
BENIN
LIBERIA
CENTRAL AFRICAN REP.
Situation in flux
CAMEROON
EQUAT. GUINEA
UGANDA
S. TOME PRINCIPE
GABON
CONGO
RWANDA
KENYA
ETHIOPIA
DJIBOUTI
FPLE (Eritrea)
FLPT
Front for the Liberation of W. Somalia
ZAIRE
BURUNDI
TANZANIA
UNITA
ANGOLA
ZAMBIA
MALAWI
MOZAMBIQUE
NAMIBIA
ZIMBABWE
BOTSWANA
SWAPO
Nat. Mozambique Front
SWAZILAND
LESOTHO
SOUTH AFRICA
ANC
MADAGASCAR

*lisario Front*: Popular front for the liberation of gui el Hamra & Rio de Oro
*NITA*: Union for the total liberation of Angola
*WAPO (Namibia)*: South West Africa People's Organization
*JC (S. Africa)*: African National Congress

Arab League
Black African nations with direct ties to the West
States under S. African influence
Pro-Soviet states
South Africa
Marxist states
Strong refugee presence
Armed political opposition

## Military Presence of the Soviets and Their Allies South of the Sahara

The only other African country where there are more than 1,500 military or civilian personnel from the Soviet bloc is the Congo. Between 1975 and 1982, the major beneficiaries of Soviet arms sales were Ethiopia, Angola, and Mozambique.

|  | USSR | Cuba | GDR* |
|---|---|---|---|
| Angola† | 700 | 18,000 | 450 |
| Ethiopia | 2,400 | 5,900 | 550 |
| Mozambique† | 500 | 1,000 | 100 |

*Source:* Department of State, Washington, DC, 1982.

---

*The German Democratic Republic generally trains police and security personnel.
†UNITA and the Mozambique National Front are supported by South Africa.

FPLE: Popular Front for the Liberation of Eritrea
FLPT: Popular Front for the Liberation of Tiger.

## French Military Presence

Military assistance agreements
Defense agreements *
French military bases ●

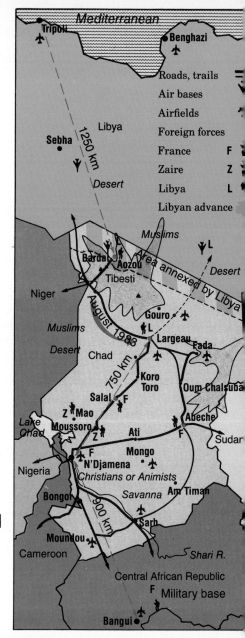

## Chad

Roads, trails
Air bases
Airfields
Foreign forces
France          F
Zaire           Z
Libya           L
Libyan advance

Military base

The military initiatives of Libya, which had already annexed unilaterally the Aozou area (100,000 sq. km.), provoked in Chad operation Manta, led by French forces (August 1983). The latter had been withdrawn in 1980 after twelve years of intervention.

Conditions in Chad (deserts, lack of water, lack of population) pose delicate and costly logistical problems for the forces present there. A prolonged "peacekeeping" situation is unfavorable to France.

# The Vulnerability of Africa
# The Military Dimensions of the French Presence in Africa

France has defense agreements with several African countries—Djibouti, Gabon, Ivory Coast, Senegal, Cameroon, Central African Republic, and Togo—and military technical assistance agreements with these same countries, plus Mauritania, Niger, Upper Volta, Benin, Congo, Madagascar, Mali, Burundi, Rwanda, and Zaire.

Agreements on joint military maneuvers are in force with Djibouti, Gabon, Ivory Coast, Senegal, Togo, and Zaire. The total number of French military advisers in Africa is close to a thousand (the largest missions are in Djibouti, Gabon, Zaire, and the Ivory Coast). There are about 7,000 troops stationed on the continent, including 3,500 in Djibouti, 1,200 in Senegal, and 1,100 in the Central African Republic. French troops have intervened several times in Africa, notably: Gabon (1964), Chad (1968–1980), Mauritania (1977–1978, air support against the Polisario), Djibouti (1976–1977), Zaire (1977–1978), and Central African Republic (1979).

During the 1970s, France withdrew militarily (after a dozen years of intervention) from Chad (1980) and from Diego-Suarez in Madagascar (1975).

At the present time, the major strategic bases in Africa are Dakar, Gabon, Central African Republic, Djibouti, and Réunion Island.

France has a 25,000-man* rapid intervention force stationed on its territory, with logistical support that has undergone continuous improvement since 1978 (the Shaba operation in Zaire). It may be that this force is currently able to intervene more rapidly than that of other powers, including the USA and the USSR.

In twenty years, French positions in Africa have suffered little erosion. In various ways, France supplies annual aid totaling nearly a billion dollars. The policy of cooperation formulated by General de Gaulle has basically continued up to the present day. These alliances, based on political, economic, and cultural interests (most are with former colonies), have been shaped over several decades by the governing elites and France and seem likely to endure.

There are about 200,000 French technical assistants in "French-speaking" Africa. In these countries, as in other African countries, France is a major arms exporter.

As for religion, the importance of Islam in northern and central Africa is great and spreading. In the southern half, Christianity is widespread. There are also numerous animists.

The states of tropical Africa are marked by religious diversity, ethnic fragmentation, and weak political structures. Except for Nigeria and Ethiopia, the states are underpopulated. These special characteristics favor ethnically based strategies, attempts at destabilization, and interventions by troops from outside the continent. Tropical Africa remains highly vulnerable.

---

*A rapid action force of about 47,000 men is being set up. It is to be used in the European theater as well.

## Angola

Railways —
S. African incursions ↑ ↑
Unstable areas

The South African forces want to create a buffer zone extending about 200 km. inside Angola so as to make the guerrilla operations of SWAPO (the Namibian liberation movement), ineffective. Pretoria supports UNITA, which is fighting the regime in Luanda.

## Zaire

Ores ■
Diamonds ▲
Copper △
Rebellion
1963–1965 ▬

Belgian interventions ✳ French interventions
(1961-1964)     (1977-1978)

Zaire was and remains the most unstable state on the continent. Between 1960 and 1965, then again in 1977 and 1978, it was the scene of outside interventions, as the West sought to protect its interests. Zaire continues to be the soft underbelly of Africa.

# Southern Africa

Southern Africa is the richest part of the continent. The apartheid system makes the situation in South Africa more conflict-laden, especially since the disappearance of Portuguese colonialism and Soviet-Cuban involvement in Angola and, to a lesser extent, in Mozambique.

In the forefront of South African concerns is the Namibian shield, rich in minerals and underpopulated. South Africa possesses there the strategic enclave of Walvis Bay. The establishment of a regime favorable to Pretoria would allow it to keep the Soviet threat in check. It is to achieve this goal that the South African army is fighting SWAPO, the Namibian liberation movement backed by Angola. SWAPO is based on the Ovambo, an ethnic group that includes some 50 percent of the black population of Namibia (totaling slightly over 1 million). For its part, South Africa is supporting UNITA, an Angolan movement based on the largest ethnic group in the country and fighting the Luanda government.

Despite widespread hostility, South Africa is continuing its military operations, punctuated by deep incursions inside southern Angola. Talks between Angola and South Africa are unlikely to change a situation fraught with the prospect of prolonged conflict.

The relatively moderate position of Mozambique, which welcomes and trains militants of the African National Congress (ANC) hostile to Pretoria, has not led to direct military action by South Africa. But South Africa supplies and supports elements of the Mozambique National Front (MNF), which is hostile to the regime.

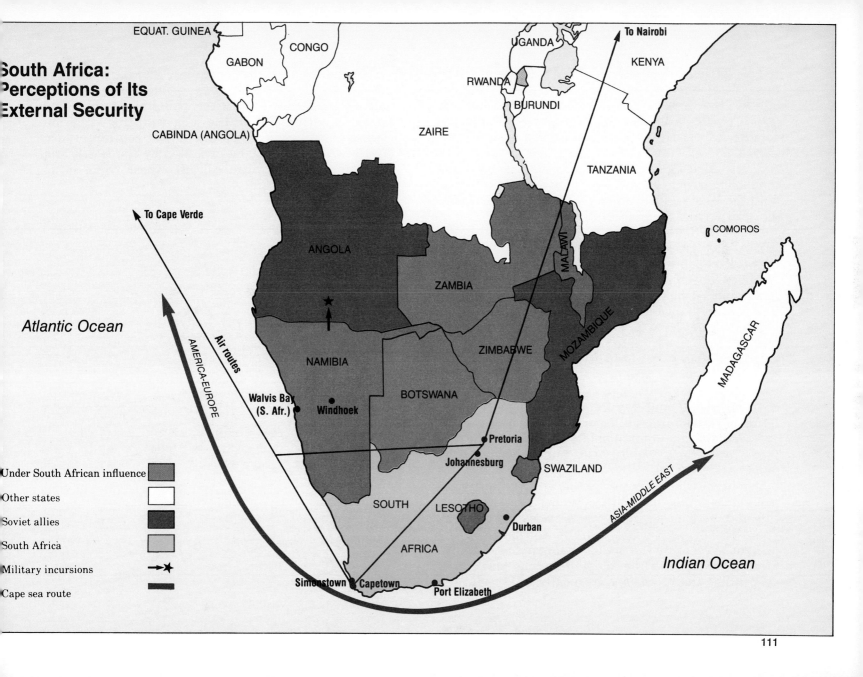

South Africa:
Perceptions of Its
External Security

EQUAT. GUINEA
GABON
CONGO
CABINDA (ANGOLA)
ZAIRE
UGANDA
RWANDA
BURUNDI
KENYA
TANZANIA
To Nairobi
Atlantic Ocean
To Cape Verde
ANGOLA
ZAMBIA
MALAWI
COMOROS
MOZAMBIQUE
AMERICA-EUROPE
Air routes
NAMIBIA
ZIMBABWE
MADAGASCAR
Walvis Bay
(S. Afr.)
Windhoek
BOTSWANA
Pretoria
Johannesburg
SWAZILAND
SOUTH
LESOTHO
Durban
ASIA-MIDDLE EAST
Indian Ocean
AFRICA
Simonstown
Capetown
Port Elizabeth

Under South African influence
Other states
Soviet allies
South Africa
Military incursions
Cape sea route

The settlement of the conflict in Zimbabwe (formerly Rhodesia) by the British and Americans rules out for the present and for domestic reasons any active participation by that country in a regional conflict, especially as it is itself faced with serious unrest.

South Africa's strength lies in its military and industrial power, as well as in its de facto alliance with the West—given, among other things, its strategic position and its mineral resources.

Since 1973, thanks to NATO equipment, South Africa has possessed at Simonstown a detection network capable of reaching Australia and South America. South Africa's power feeds on the military and economic weakness of its adversaries. The frontline states (Tanzania, Botswana, Zambia, Mozambique, Angola) have no means of changing the status quo.

Despite theoretical hostility, trade between South Africa and several African states (Kenya, Zaire, Malawi, etc.) is far from insignificant. South Africa is, however, still a long way from organizing a "constellation of states" around Pretoria.

Apartheid, an unjustifiable system, gives advantages to Pretoria's adversaries and undermines its diplomatic position.

The numerical weakness of the white minority (15 percent) remains the Achilles' heel of the system, and this minority is declining proportionately year by year. Pretoria's racial strategy consists for the present in coopting the nonblack minorities (Indians, Malays, coloreds) while keeping out the blacks and deepending their divisions ethnically and juridically.

This policy seems to be too late and to involve too few changes. It is true that the principle of "one man, one vote" would lead to the political death of the white minority. But in the long run, this situation can only lead to increasingly violent confrontations. These will, of course, be exploited by the USSR and its allies in an African context where there is no support for apartheid.

## South Africa

| | Percent of World Production | Reserves |
|---|---|---|
| Gold | 51% | Important reserves |
| Chromium | 34 | 67% |
| Manganese | 23 | 41 |
| Vanadium | 30 | 42 |
| Platinum | 45 | 81 |
| Antimony | 16 | 7 |
| Ilmenite | | 15 |
| Rutile | | 4 |
| Asbestos | 6 | 21 |
| Diamonds | 18 | |
| Nickel | 3 | |
| Coal | 4 | |
| Uranium | 14 | 11 |

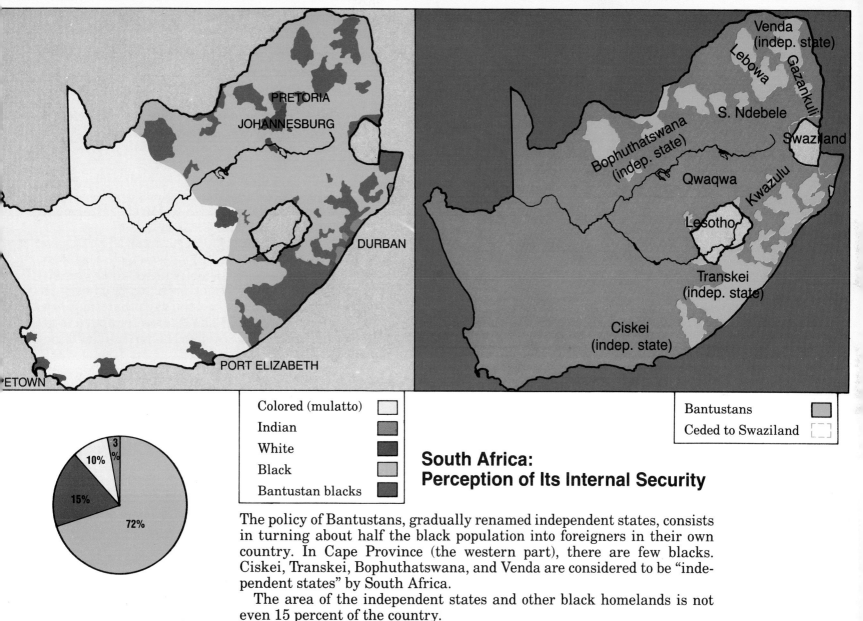

PRETORIA
JOHANNESBURG
DURBAN
PORT ELIZABETH
ETOWN

Venda
(indep. state)
Lebowa
Gazankuli
S. Ndebele
Bophuthatswana
(indep. state)
Swaziland
Qwaqwa
Kwazulu
Lesotho
Transkei
(indep. state)
Ciskei
(indep. state)

Colored (mulatto)
Indian
White
Black
Bantustan blacks

Bantustans
Ceded to Swaziland

3%
10%
15%
72%

## South Africa:
## Perception of Its Internal Security

The policy of Bantustans, gradually renamed independent states, consists in turning about half the black population into foreigners in their own country. In Cape Province (the western part), there are few blacks. Ciskei, Transkei, Bophuthatswana, and Venda are considered to be "independent states" by South Africa.

The area of the independent states and other black homelands is not even 15 percent of the country.

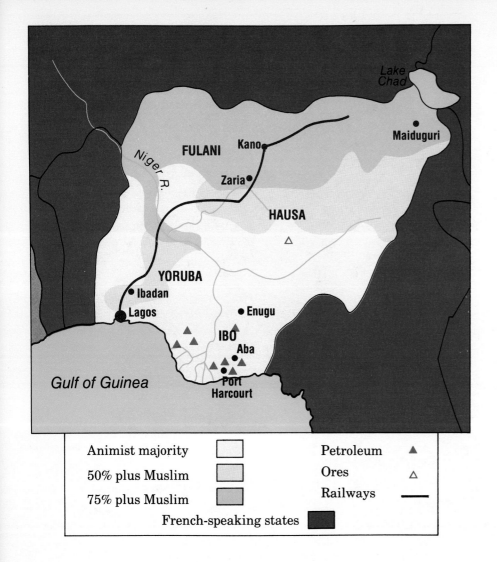

**Animist majority**

**50% plus Muslim**

**75% plus Muslim**

**French-speaking states**

**Petroleum** ▲

**Ores** △

**Railways** —

# Nigeria: A Regional Power in Tropical Africa

Nigeria is the only state that can aspire to be a regional power in tropical Africa, and it is also the most populous country in Africa (about 90 million inhabitants).

The republic's federal system seeks to resolve the ethnic and religious problems that were largely responsible for the attempted Biafran secession (1967–1970).

With its large oil resources, Nigeria saw real growth in the 1970s, which enabled it to play a continent-wide political role. The direct impact of Nigeria on its neighbors is partly hampered by the fact that they are French-speaking. The relatively rapid end of the oil boom has brought Nigeria, like all the populous oil states, back to its former difficulties, as was shown by the expulsion of 2 million foreign immigrant workers to neighboring countries in 1983.

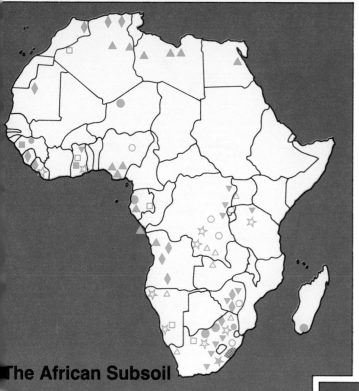

## The African Subsoil

| | | | |
|---|---|---|---|
| Petroleum | ▲ | Bauxite | ■ |
| Uranium | ● | Manganese | □ |
| Copper | △ | Tin | ○ |
| Iron | ◆ | Platinum | ★ |
| Chrome | ● | Diamonds | ☆ |
| Gold | ▼ | Coal | ⬤ |

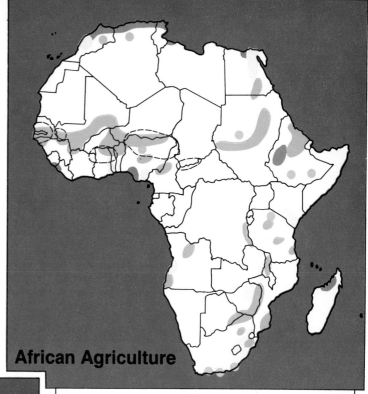

## African Agriculture

| | | | |
|---|---|---|---|
| Barley | ▨ | Rice | ▨ |
| Sheep | ● | Wheat, corn | ☐ |
| Peanuts | ◯ | Millet, sorghum | ▨ |

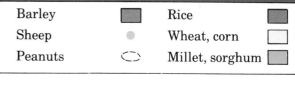

Sahel

LDCs ☐

## The Less Developed Countries

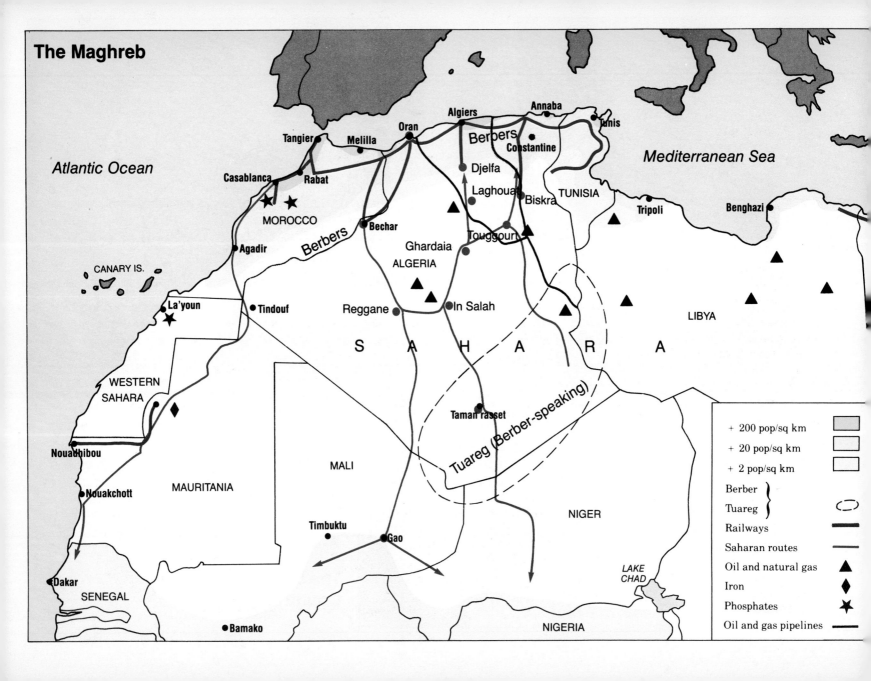

# The Maghreb

*Atlantic Ocean*

*Mediterranean Sea*

Tangier
Melilla
Oran
Algiers
Annaba
Tunis
Berbers
Constantine

Casablanca
Rabat
Djelfa
Laghouat
Biskra
TUNISIA
Tripoli
Benghazi

MOROCCO
Berbers

Agadir
Bechar
Ghardaia
ALGERIA
Touggourt

CANARY IS.

La'youn
Tindouf
Reggane
In Salah
LIBYA

S  A  H  A  R  A

WESTERN
SAHARA
Taman rasset

Nouadhibou
Tuareg (Berber-speaking)

MALI
NIGER

MAURITANIA
Nouakchott

Timbuktu
Gao
LAKE
CHAD

Dakar
SENEGAL
Bamako
NIGERIA

| | | |
|---|---|---|
| + 200 pop/sq km | | ▨ |
| + 20 pop/sq km | | ▢ |
| + 2 pop/sq km | | ▢ |
| Berber ⎫ | | |
| Tuareg ⎬ | | ⬭ |
| Railways | | ▬▬▬ |
| Saharan routes | | ─── |
| Oil and natural gas | | ▲ |
| Iron | | ◆ |
| Phosphates | | ★ |
| Oil and gas pipelines | | ─── |

The Maghreb extends, geographically, from Mauritania to Libya. It is peopled by Arab Berbers and has more than 50 million inhabitants, most of whom are concentrated in the coastal strip or on the slopes of the Atlas Mountains. After southern Africa, it is the richest region in Africa (oil and gas, phosphates, iron).

Maghreb unity, although an oft-proclaimed goal, remains in the realm of the hypothetical, and has been dominated for the last two decades by the rivalry between Morocco and Algeria, further fueled by the conflict in and over Western Sahara. One of the issues at stake in this conflict is dominance in the Maghreb. Morocco would win a virtual monopoly on the world supply of phosphates (outside the USA and the USSR); Algeria would obtain indirect access to the Atlantic and at the same time finally destroy Moroccan dreams of a "Greater Morocco."

Western Sahara (256,000 sq. km.) has the distinction of being the only decolonized African territory (in addition to Eritrea) not to have gained independence automatically. The Polisario Front, set up in 1973, first fought Spanish colonialism. In 1975, basing itself on what it asserted were its historical rights, Morocco occupied two-thirds of the then Spanish Sahara, from which Madrid had just withdrawn. Mauritania occupied a third of the country (1975–1979), and then gave it up. Heavily supported by Algeria, the Polisario carried on an effective guerrilla war (1976–1982), and won recognition, thanks to Algeria, from a large number of members of the OAU as the representative of the Saharan Arab Democratic Republic. Neither the USA nor the USSR recognizes the SADR. France supports the idea of a referendum.

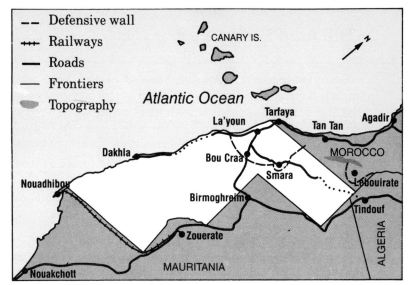

## Western Sahara

*The erection of a wall (1979) marking off the useful part of the country has turned out to be militarily effective.*

Given the prevalence of nomadism and the number of refugees outside its borders, such a referendum would be likely to be disputed. The last Spanish census gave 73,500 inhabitants. A realistic estimate would put the figure between 100,000 and 150,000.*

Libya, a rich oil state that is very underpopulated, lacks the manpower to fulfill the ambitions of Colonel Qadafi. It has confined itself to the role of troublemaker, both in the Arab world and along the edges of the Sahara. The USSR is active there. Apart from Libya, all the Maghreb states send a substantial proportion of their workers to European countries.

---

*The Polisario Front gives a figure of 300,000 Sahrawis.

# The Arab Middle East

As an intermediate zone between Europe, Asia, and black Africa, the Arab world enjoys the advantage of being situated on major transport routes, but it also suffers the vulnerability this gives rise to. Since World War II the strategic and economic importance of this vital area has been continuously at the center of world tensions.

The creation of Israel (1948), a consequence of modern nationalism, anti-Semitism, and the genocide of the Jews, led to Arab rejection of European interference. From 1967, Palestinian nationalism has made its presence felt and raises not only the refugee problem, but also that of the necessity for a separate state.

The Arab world, confronted by an industrialized Israeli nation that possesses a modern army and is supported by the USA, has been mobilized and inspired around slogans of unity and demands for a Palestinian state.

The Arab countries, whose political autonomy was limited until 1952 and even until 1958, progressively built up their strength until, from 1973 onward, they became an economic and financial factor in the world balance of power. Nationalism, which used to be predominantly socialistic (Nasserism and Baathism), has today become conservative, partly because of the place occupied by Saudi Arabia. Militarily, the neutralization of Egypt (1978) gave a decisive boost to Israeli superiority. The PLO lacks both the strength to impose its demands and the means to negotiate (negotiation being seen as treason).

Israel, obsessed with security and enjoying military superiority, has annexed the Golan Heights (which belonged to Syria) and, by multiplying its settlements, demonstrated its determination to retain the West Bank (Judea and Samaria). The number of Palestinians under Israeli jurisdiction is about 2 million (of whom 1.4 million are in the occupied territories), as against 3 million Jewish Israelis.

The Arab world has vast mineral resources: more than 50 percent of world oil reserves and 25 percent of gas reserves, a third of the world's phosphate, and an abundance of several vital minerals. The agricultural sector remains weak. Above all, too few concerted efforts seem to have been made to take maximum advantage of the financial resources at its disposal to lay the foundations for real agricultural and industrial development.

Islam, "religion and way of life," proclaims itself to be a social and cultural fact defining every aspect of behavior. It is interpreted today not only as a religion, but also as a national value. Only rarely is it not the state religion. National values have often been given pride of place when modern Arab nationalism has asserted itself. In periods of crisis like today, fundamentalism exercises a growing influence.

Religious sects continue to evoke strong feelings of belonging. In Syria, for example, state power is tightly controlled by the Alawite minority, in Iraq by the Arab Sunni minority.

Baathist Syria, rival of the no less Baathist Iraq, an ally of the USSR, is isolated. It has failed to bring to fruition its plans for a Greater Syria, including dragging Lebanon and Jordan into its orbit. The essential problem of the government there appears to be self-preservation.

Jordan has steadily strengthened itself over the last decade both militarily and economically, thanks largely to American aid. Although often threatened, it has succeeded in surviving, thanks to the political skill and determination of King Hussein. The Hashemite kingdom is in a peculiar situation in that two-thirds of its population is Palestinian. A federal Jordanian–Palestinian arrangement has often been proposed. Among other things, it would involve Israeli withdrawal from the West Bank, and that seems most unlikely.

The region's strategic importance involves Great Power support from the nations' respective allies. Despite the efforts of the USSR, the USA has managed to retain its predominance in the region. Its problem remains to reconcile, insofar as that is possible, the divergent aspirations regarding the Palestinian problem and the status of Jerusalem of its Israeli ally, on the one hand, and on the other, of its Arab allies, especially Saudi Arabia.

Given that a settlement of the Palestinian problem seems unlikely, the prospects of continuing conflict in the Middle East remain great.

The League of Arab Nations: Created in 1945, it comprises all 21 Arab states except Western Sahara (formerly Spanish). It includes one non-Arab state, Somalia. The PLO (Palestinian Liberation Organization) is, in fact, an equal member. Many economic associations reinforce cooperation.

# Islam and Religious Sects in the Middle East

| Christians | ∵ |
| Shiite Muslims | |
| Sunni Muslims | |
| Sunni-Shiite overlap | //// |

Muslim Sects

Wahhabites (W)

Alawites (A)

Druse (D)

Zaidites (Z)

Sanoussis (S)

Mahadis (M)

Ismailis (I)

Kharijites (K)

**The Fertile Middle East**

Cultivated areas
Fertile Crescent

**Sparse Populations**

More than 100 pop/sq km
10-100 pop/sq km

**A Major Resource: Oil**

Petroleum ▲
Oil pipelines ——

**Land and Water**

| | % Land Under Cultivation | % Irrigated Cultivated Land |
|---|---|---|
| Iran | 14 | 20 |
| Turkey | 34 | 7 |
| Israel | 20 | 40 |
| Saudi Arabia | 1 | 80 |
| Egypt | 2.5 | 100 |
| Iraq | 18 | 50 |
| Libya | 2 | 9 |
| Syria | 35 | 10 |
| Lebanon | 27 | 20 |
| Jordan | 11 | 7 |
| Yemen | 7 | 10 |
| South Yemen | 1 | 80 |
| Kuwait | 1 | 100 |
| United Arab Emirates | 5 | 100 |
| Oman | 1 | — |
| Mean | 11 | 24 |

**Oil in the Gulf***

| Production 1981 | | Reserves (54% of world total) |
|---|---|---|
| Saudi Arabia | 63.6% | 46% |
| Emirates | 9.7% | 9% |
| Iran | 8.5% | 16% |
| Kuwait | 7.5% | 15% |
| Iraq | 5.8% | 9% |
| Qatar | 2.5% | 1% |
| Oman | 2.0% | 0.5% |
| Bahrain | 0.4% | 0.1% |

*The Gulf contains 25% of the world reserves of natural gas.

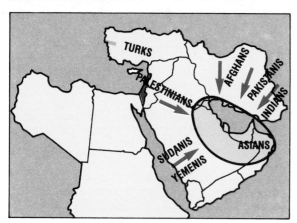

# Immigration into the Gulf

Thanks to various means of fuel conservation and substitution, the West has succeeded, in ten years, in reducing its oil consumption by about 25 percent.

Oil production had to be progressively reduced after 1979–1980. In 1983, oil prices fell. Over the decade 1973 to 1983, the percentage of oil coming from the Gulf was 30 percent for the USA, 60 percent for Western Europe, and 70 percent for Japan.

### Population of the Arabian Peninsula (in millions)

| | |
|---|---|
| Saudi Arabia | 10.4 |
| Yemen | 5.8 |
| South Yemen | 2.0 |
| Kuwait | 1.4 |
| Oman | 0.9 |
| Emirates | 0.8 |
| Bahrain | 0.4 |
| Qatar | 0.2 |
| **Total** | **21.9** |

### Foreign Skilled Personnel and Labor in the Arab Gulf States

| | Total Employed | Foreign Employed | % |
|---|---|---|---|
| Saudi Arabia | 2,384,000 | 1,300,000 | 57 |
| Bahrain | 60,000 | 30,000 | 50 |
| Emirates | 300,000 | 239,000 | 80 |
| Kuwait | 304,000 | 211,000 | 75 |
| Oman | 350,000 | 70,000 | 20 |
| Qatar | 86,000 | 54,000 | 80 |

**Origins:**

Yemenis
Palestinians } 75%
Egyptians
Jordanians

Pakistanis
Indians } 25%
Other Asian countries

The Arabian Peninsula is the most vulnerable region in the Gulf. Five states combined (including those grouped in the United Arab Emirates) do not have more than 4 million inhabitants. It was essentially to guarantee the stability of Saudi Arabia and these five states that the American Rapid Deployment Force was set up. Part of this force can be deployed from Diego Garcia (3,700 km. from the Gulf), with facilities at the air and naval bases at Masirah (Oman), Berbera (Somalia), and Mombasa (Kenya). The main drawback of the RDF at present lies in the excessively long time required to intervene (between 3 and 7 days for the first forces). The very idea of this force seems too ponderous and powerful, for lightning operations are infinitely more likely than an intervention of conventional dimensions.

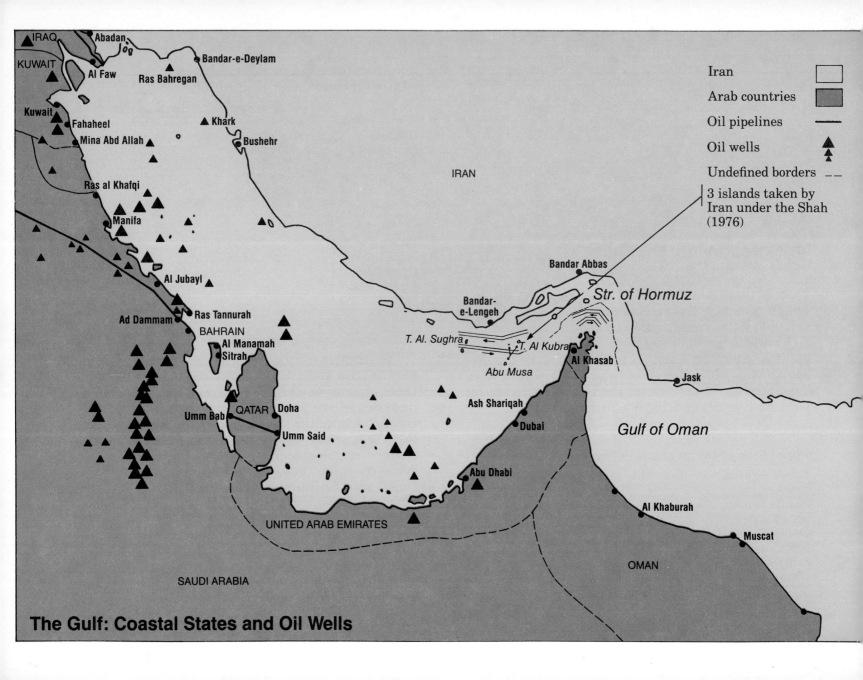

The Gulf: Coastal States and Oil Wells

# Saudi Arabia

In November 1973, Saudi Arabia reduced its oil output by 30 percent and soon after quadrupled the price. In a year, its GNP rose 250 percent. Since 1974, Saudi Arabia's position, which had already been rising after 1967, has become preeminent. During the previous decade, the Wahhabite kingdom, founded on fundamentalist Islam and enduring tribal structures, had been mainly preoccupied in foiling attempted revolutions deriving from Middle East socialism and Nasserism in particular. Egypt's defeat in 1967, then Sadat's rise to power and the break with the USSR (1972), which it encouraged, enabled Saudi Arabia to go on the offensive as leader of the conservative forces in the Arab Middle East.

Although it has increased its capabilities, particularly its air power (air base at Tabuk, not far from Israel), Saudi Arabia remains a second-rank military power. The leaders of a kingdom that is underpopulated (about 10 million inhabitants), fabulously rich, and sharply stratified, in the middle of an unstable and coveted region, are obsessed with security and stability. Political control is highly centralized and tight, reinforced by the peculiar harshness of Wahhabism. The royal family (which is very large) incarnates the regime, and fears both any significant change in the world market that might precipitate a depression, and the effects of rapid modernization in a society built on traditional religious and tribal values. The occupation of the Great Mosque in Mecca in 1979 was a sign of the relative fragility of the regime. The proportion of immigrant labor is high, although it is split into various ethnic groups and is frequently rotated.

Externally, the Soviet presence in the Red Sea and the pro-Soviet revolutionary center in South Yemen are perceived as serious threats. The southern frontier is strategically vulnerable.

Saudi Arabia is too weak militarily to influence its neighbors, but uses its vast financial resources as a means of foreign policy. Its aid, very large in volume, is used to ensure the stability of friendly neighboring Arab regimes, to help the Arab states generally (in their struggle with Israel among other things), to combat vigorously any Communist influence, and to encourage Muslim states throughout the world (including those of Africa and Southeast Asia) to strengthen the place of Islam in state and society. More ambitiously, Saudi Arabia is attempting as much as possible to maintain the stability of the world market, hence its moderating role in OPEC. In this respect, alliance with the USA is seen as vital, and the interests of the two states converge (except over Israel). In a period when dangers are increasing everywhere, internal, regional, and world stability are at the center of Saudi preoccupations.

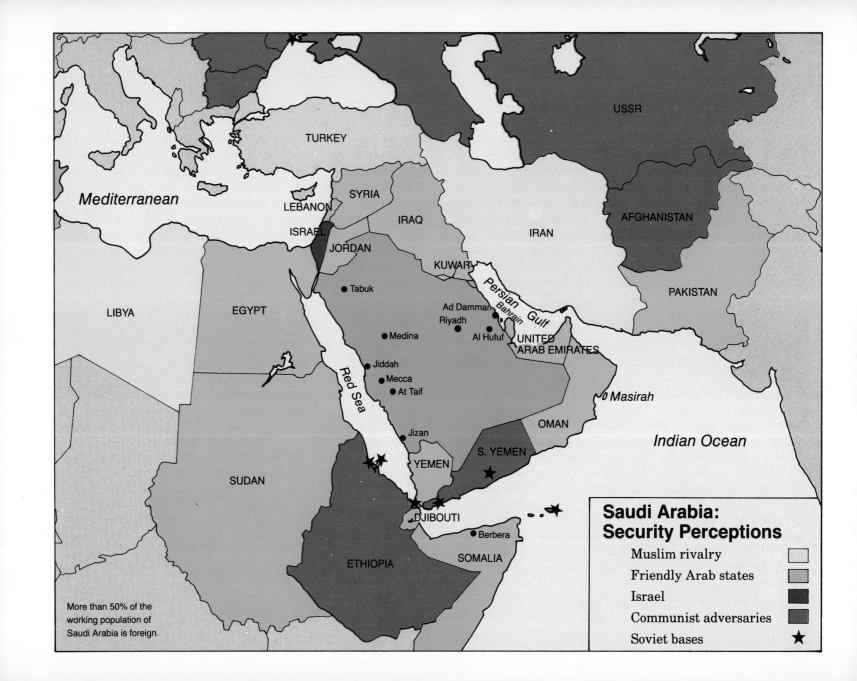

**Saudi Arabia: Security Perceptions**

Muslim rivalry

Friendly Arab states

Israel

Communist adversaries

Soviet bases ★

More than 50% of the working population of Saudi Arabia is foreign.

Mediterranean

USSR

TURKEY

SYRIA

LEBANON

ISRAEL

JORDAN

IRAQ

IRAN

AFGHANISTAN

KUWAIT

PAKISTAN

Persian Gulf

Tabuk

Ad Damman

Bahrain

Riyadh

Medina

Al Hufuf

UNITED ARAB EMIRATES

Jiddah

Mecca

At Taif

Masirah

LIBYA

EGYPT

Red Sea

Jizan

OMAN

Indian Ocean

YEMEN

S. YEMEN

SUDAN

DJIBOUTI

Berbera

SOMALIA

ETHIOPIA

## EGYPT UNDER NASSER

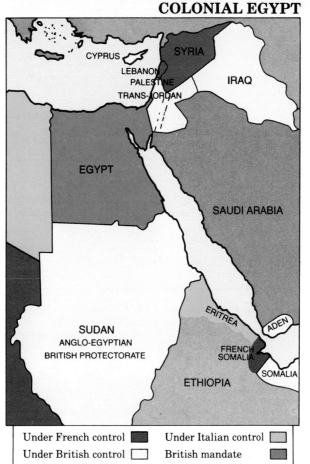

CYPRUS · SYRIA · LEBANON · USA 1958 → · Suez 1956 · JORDAN · IRAQ · Cairo · ISRAEL · KUWAIT · LIBYA · EGYPT · SAUDI ARABIA · SUDAN · YEMEN · ETHIOPIA · ADEN

Members UAR ▢ Suez conflict →
Other Arab states ▢ Lebanon (US interv.) →

## COLONIAL EGYPT

CYPRUS · SYRIA · LEBANON · PALESTINE · TRANS-JORDAN · IRAQ · EGYPT · SAUDI ARABIA · SUDAN ANGLO-EGYPTIAN BRITISH PROTECTORATE · ERITREA · ADEN · FRENCH SOMALIA · SOMALIA · ETHIOPIA

Under French control ■    Under Italian control ▨
Under British control ▢    British mandate ▨

## EGYPT'S GEOPOLITICAL LOGIC

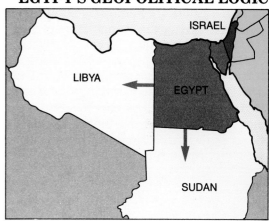

ISRAEL · LIBYA ← EGYPT → · SUDAN

# Egypt

Egypt is the center of the Arab world: It is the most populous Arab state—one third of all Arabs are Egyptians—and it is also the most ancient and most homogeneous nation in the Arab world, with the largest agricultural population in the Middle East. In spite of very limited resources, Egypt remains, be-cause of its population, a key factor in the Middle Eastern balance.

In Nasser's time, attempts at Arab unity brought Egypt and Syria together in the United Arab Repub-lic (1958–1961), which in 1963 added Iraq and Yemen. These alliances were short-lived.

Considering its regional geopolitical interests rather than the utopia of pan-Arabism, Egypt should logically direct its efforts in the direction of Sudan (with its fertile, underpopulated lands) and Libya, rich in oil and very sparsely populated.

Today, since the conclusion of the peace treaty (1978) that enabled Egypt to regain Sinai (1982), Cairo has taken up a neutral position in possible future Arab–Israeli conflicts. The American alliance and Saudi aid seem unlikely to resolve the crisis of Egyptian society (in part a demographic one), any more than Nasserite "socialism" did before them. Geopolitical ambitions could in future appear as a solution, if the regional situation allows it.

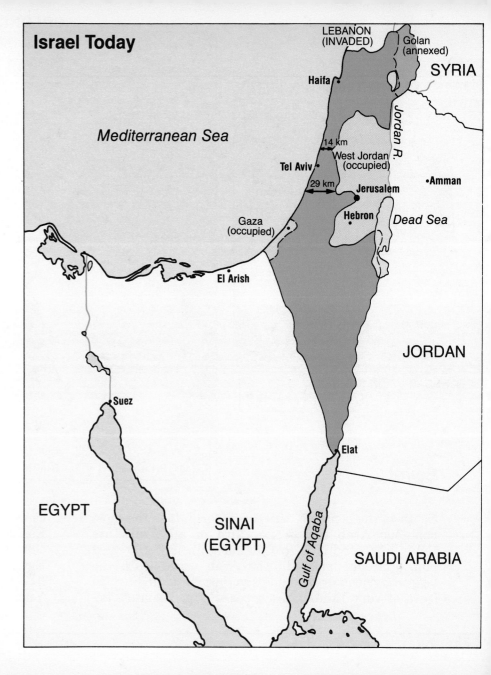

**Israel Today**

LEBANON (INVADED)
Golan (annexed)
SYRIA
Haifa
Mediterranean Sea
Jordan R.
14 km
West Jordan (occupied)
Tel Aviv
•Amman
29 km
Jerusalem
Hebron
Dead Sea
Gaza (occupied)
El Arish
JORDAN
Suez
Elat
EGYPT
SINAI (EGYPT)
Gulf of Aqaba
SAUDI ARABIA

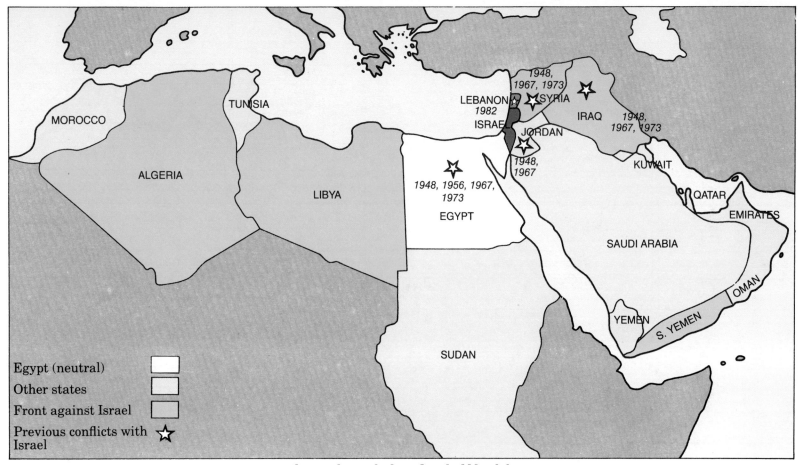

**Israel and the Arab World**

The agreement among some Arab countries never to recognize Israel, set up in December 1977, includes: Algeria, Libya, Syria, South Yemen, Iraq, and the PLO.*

According to UNRRA, there are 1,925,762 Palestinian refugees (1982). The Palestinian diaspora is estimated to number 2 million:

| | |
|---|---|
| Jordan | 920,000 |
| Lebanon | 420,000 |
| Syria | 250,000 |
| Kuwait | 200,000 |
| Others | 250,000 |

---

*Iraq's participation in the 1967 and 1973 wars was limited.

127

**Palestine 1947 Jewish Settlements**

Tel Aviv
Jaffa
Amman
Beersheba

**Jewish State 1947 UN Plan**

Tel Aviv
Jaffa
Jerusalem
Amman
Beersheba

**Israel 1949**

Damascus
Kesar Blum
Haifa
Tel Aviv
Amman
Beersheba
Beersheba
Elat

**Israel after 1967 and Occupied Territories**

Golan
Haifa
Tel Aviv
Jerusalem
Gaza
Beersheba
Sinai
Elat

Old City
Muslim quarter
Christian quarter
Moria
Armenian quarter
Jewish quarter

Armistice line (1949)
Mount Scopus
Tel Aviv
Mandelbaum Gate
No man's land 1949-1967
Mount of Olive
Old City
Jerich
No man's land 1948-1967
Demilitarized (1949-1967)
Armistice line (1949)
Bethlehem
**Jerusalem**
**(before 1967**

**Israeli Withdrawal
from Sinai
(1978–1982)**

**Principal Palestinian
Refugee Camps ★**

**Israeli Settlements:
West Bank and
Golan Heights ★**

**Lebanon, early 1982**

Legend:
- Haddad enclave
- Syrian occupation
- Palestinian-Leftist Leb.
- Christians-Phalangists
- UN forces

**Lebanon, June 1982**

Legend:
- Israeli advance
- Syrian forces
- Christians-Phalangists

**Lebanon, July 1983, after the Israeli Retreat**

Legend:
- Syrian forces
- Israeli forces
- Israeli retreat
- Lebanese zone

After the removal of Palestinian organizations from Jordan (September 1970), most Palestinian forces regrouped in Lebanon, militarily the weakest state in the region. Their presence broke the fragile Lebanese communal and political balance. Civil war broke out in 1975 and allowed Syria to intervene (1976), fatally weakening Lebanese sovereignty, which rapidly disintegrated into various spheres of influence. Internal confrontations resulted in de facto partitions.

Israeli intervention (1982) as far as Beirut altered the relations of force inside the country by mandating the withdrawal of PLO forces. The sovereignty of the Lebanese state for the time being is purely nominal, and antagonisms are still very much alive. The laborious negotiations on the withdrawal of Israeli troops from Lebanon enables the much more important problem for Israel—the status of the West Bank and the future of its settlements—to be postponed.

**Beirut, October 1983**

**Lebanon and Its Environment**

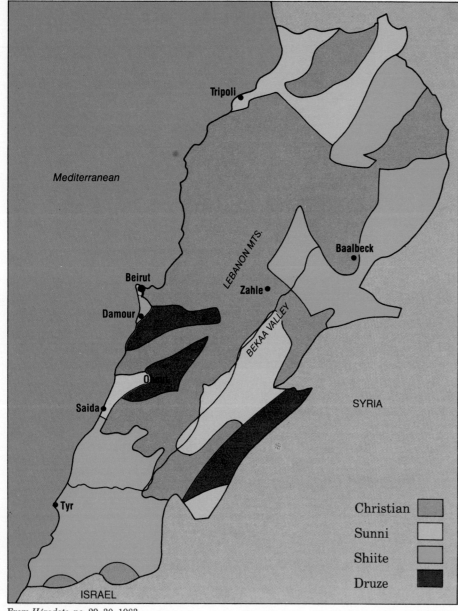

From *Hérodote*, no. 29–30, 1983.

## Principal Religious Communities of Lebanon

| Community | Population |
|---|---|
| Shiite | about 600,000 to 650,000 |
| Maronite | about 550,000 to 600,000 |
| Sunni | about 500,000 |
| Greek Orthodox | about 250,000 to 280,000 |
| Greek Catholic | about 200,000 to 220,000 |
| Druze | about 150,000 to 180,000 |

- The figures given here for communities active as such in actual conflicts are estimates where there are no recent census data for these religious sects.
- The Shiites are spread out over a good part of the country in scattered settlements. Most are rural people.
- The Sunni are traditionally city people (Beirut, Tripoli, Saida). They occupy rural areas near the cities, as well as the Bekaa Valley.
- The Greek Orthodox and Greek Catholic communities are made up of Arabs Christianized over the centuries. They are traditionally city people, especially the Greek Orthodox group.
- The mountains of Lebanon and other hilly areas have historically been places of refuge for two threatened communities: the Maronite Christians and the Druze (a dissident sect of Islam). The Maronite villages are located on the exit routes from the cities as well as on the mountain routes. The Druze, in addition to the mountains, occupy the Shouf and Mt. Hermon.

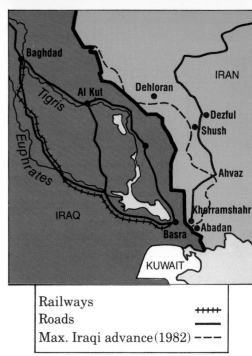

**The Iran-Iraq Conflict**

Legend:
- Petroleum
- Iraq
- Soviets
- Arabs

Railways ++++
Roads ———
Max. Iraqi advance (1982) – – –

## Iran's Perception of External Threats

The fall of the Shah after a popular revolution (1979) deprived the United States of a major ally in the region. None of the forces opposing the government of Khomeini and the mullahs has been able to gain widespread support, and the masses of the population continue to support a regime that seems destined to last, no doubt even after the disappearance of its charismatic leader.

But hostility toward the United States should not obscure the fact that it is with the Soviet Union that Iran has a long common frontier, and that its sovereignty was for a long time a matter of dispute between Russia and Great Britain, which even drew up a proposal for partition (1907). Moreover, by moving into Afghanistan, the USSR now adjoins Iran's eastern frontier.

133

As early as 1979, the Kurds (Sunni Muslims) demanded autonomy within the framework of Iran; they established this autonomy de facto and have maintained it since by force of arms. Most Iranians, welded together by Shiism and by Persian culture, both expressions of their identity, and fired by revolutionary ardor and/or the climate of the "fatherland in danger," offered fierce resistance to the Iraqi invasion (1980), helped by their heavy numerical superiority (3 to 1).

## Iran–Iraq Conflict

The rivalry between Iraq and Iran (which for a long time supported Iraqi Kurds fighting the central government) was fueled by concessions Iraq was obliged to make to Iran in 1975 (the Algiers agreements) leading to withdrawal of Iran's support for the Kurds, and their eventual collapse. These concessions involved problems of sovereignty in the Shatt-al-Arab and the Iraqi claim to the ethnically Arab Iranian province of Khuzistan.

Capitalizing on the restoration of peace and the considerable increase in oil revenues, Saddam Hussein, the Iraqi strong man in a regime which, since 1968, had devoted itself to building and consolidating the state, launched an ambitious development program in Iraq.

Hussein took advantage of the disorder created by the revolutionary process in Iran and sought, by invading Iran, to make Iraq the leading regional power in the Middle East. Failing to utilize the strategy of the rapid tank-led offensive, Iraq became bogged down in a war of attrition. Although the Iraqi people were not very enthusiastic about this military adventure, the majority, who are Shiite, ignored the calls to revolt issued by Ayatollah Khomeini.

After two years, and despite great logistical and supply difficulties, the Iranian forces succeeded in turning the situation around. But, having invaded Iraq, the Iranians in turn became bogged down. The Baath party's organization (some 400,000 members) appears likely to hold up, while external assistance (from France* and the Arab countries, including Saudi Arabia) is assured.

No state (except Syria and Israel) wants the collapse of the Iraqi regime and a change in the balance in Iran's favor. Whatever the outcome, the economic consequences of the conflict, not to mention the human losses, have been heavy for both countries.

*In the autumn of 1983, France delivered five Super-Etendards to Iraq.

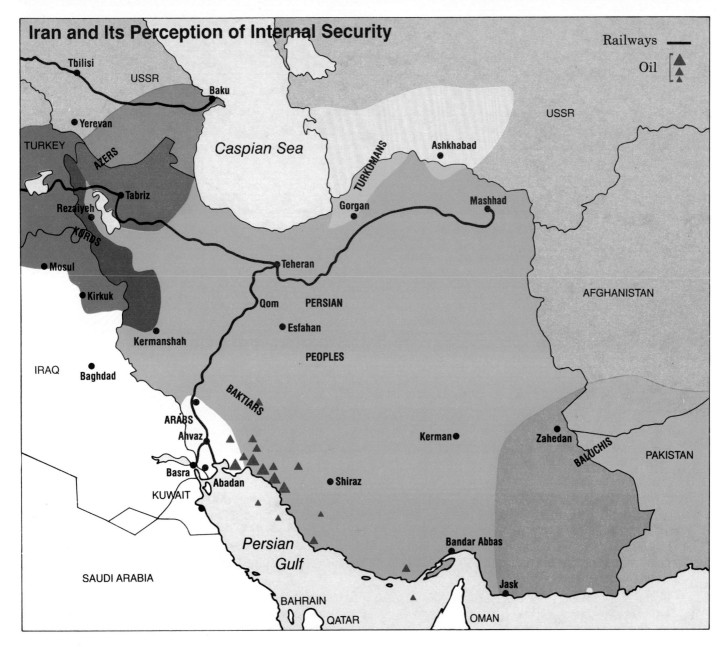

# Iran and Its Perception of Internal Security

Railways ——
Oil

Tbilisi
USSR
Baku
Yerevan
Caspian Sea
USSR
TURKEY
AZERS
Ashkhabad
TURKOMANS
Tabriz
Gorgan
Mashhad
Rezaiyeh
KURDS
Mosul
Teheran
AFGHANISTAN
Kirkuk
Qom
PERSIAN
Kermanshah
Esfahan
IRAQ
PEOPLES
Baghdad
BAKTIARS
ARABS
Kerman
Zahedan
Ahvaz
BALUCHIS
PAKISTAN
Basra
Shiraz
Abadan
KUWAIT
Persian
Gulf
Bandar Abbas
SAUDI ARABIA
Jask
BAHRAIN
QATAR
OMAN

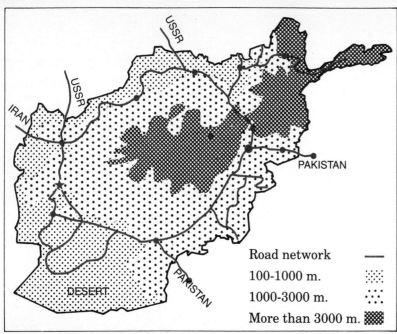

**TOPOGRAPHY: AN OBSTACLE TO COMMUNICATIONS**

Road network ———
100-1000 m. (dotted)
1000-3000 m. (dotted)
More than 3000 m. (hatched)

**A MOSAIC OF PEOPLES**

Baluchis
Uzbeks
Tadjiks
Hazaras
Pathans
Turkomans

# Afghanistan

The Soviet intervention in Afghanistan is the first Soviet intervention outside the Warsaw Pact countries since the beginning of the Cold War.

The government that emerged from the Marxist-Leninist-inspired coup d'état (1978) rapidly ran up against a massive uprising with many different causes. The Soviet occupation is facilitated by the fact that the two countries share a common border. The USSR's intervention comes on top of Soviet initiatives in Angola (1975) and Ethiopia (1977), which took advantage of strategic vacuums and the weakening of American will after the war in Vietnam and the fall of the Shah (1979).

Afghanistan's traditional buffer-state role is a thing of the past. The USSR has now brought Afghanistan within its camp. Soviet troops will not withdraw from a country deemed to be part of the geostrategic space of the USSR.*

*The time when the USSR had to leave Iranian Azerbaijan (1946) is past.

Badly organized but highly motivated, the Afghan rebels, supported by the population, hold the countryside, have external assistance, and all the support required for long-term resistance.

Pakistan is the logistical base of the resistance; it has received 3 million refugees* and is particularly vulnerable, although it is supported by the USA and China as well as by Saudi Arabia.

By occupying Afghanistan, the Soviets have totally transformed Pakistan's security perception, which previously was focused on its rivalry with India.

---

*The official figure of 4 million seems much too high.

## Turkey

With a thirty-year lead over Nasserite Egypt, the Turks, after the collapse of an Ottoman Empire undermined by national issues, succeeded, thanks to Mustapha Kemal and a military organization based on a traditional state, in avoiding subjugation. Modern Turkey, the first truly independent nation-state in the Afro-Asian world after Japan, was established. But modernization consisted mostly of the external forms of European institutions and not their economic bases, while the nation remained handicapped by a traditional, "backward" society.

Turkey, a member of NATO, the OECD, and the Council of Europe, is the only state in the Middle East linked to the West by a military pact. Turkey seeks to be European and wants to join the Common Market. In the Middle East its imperial past, its peculiarities, and its political leanings isolate it from its neighbors.

It is the only country in the Middle East outside of Egypt to recognize the state of Israel. Traditionally, the main enemy of the Turks is "the Moscof" (the Russian). The Turkish elites have long been aware of the importance their northern neighbor attaches to the vital geostrategic position of Asia Minor. The fall of the Shah of Iran, which deprived the United States of a major regional ally, increased the value of the alliance with Turkey and the inclination of the West (especially the United States and West Germany) to contribute economic assistance to a country whose stability is necessary to NATO.

**Turkey: Perception of Threats**

| Railways | ▬▬▬ |
|---|---|
| USSR and allies | |
| Greece (antagonistic) | |
| Arab countries | |
| Kurds | |

After the defeat of the Ottoman Empire, a short-lived Armenian republic was set up and recognized within frontiers laid down by President Wilson (in the years 1915–1917, some 1 million Armenians died during deportations ordered by the Young Turks). The Kurds seemed likely to win autonomous status. The Greeks invaded Anatolia.

## Turkey in 1920

| | |
|---|---|
| Turkey (Sèvres Treaty 1920) | |
| Armenia | |
| Occupied by Greece | |
| Occupied by France and Italy | |
| Ceded to France | |
| Ceded to Britain | |
| Area planned for Kurdish autonomy | |

## Birth of Modern Turkey (1919–1922)

Modern Turkey was built on the annihilation of the Armenians and the reconquest of northeastern Anatolia, the expulsion of the Greeks in Asia Minor after their defeat (followed by an exchange of populations), and a process of integration/repression of a large Kurdish minority deprived of all rights as an ethnic group.

**The Ottoman Empire in 1914**

## Cyprus

Turkish intervention in Cyprus (1974), where the Greek (82 percent) and Turkish (18 percent) communities were fighting each other, revived a multifaceted dispute between Greece and Turkey—both members of NATO. This dispute especially concerns Turkish claims to the continental shelf of the Aegean Sea.

| | |
|---|---|
| Greek control | |
| Turkish control | |
| Dividing line | |
| Turkish communities | |

## Ethiopia, the Muslim World, and the Soviet Presence

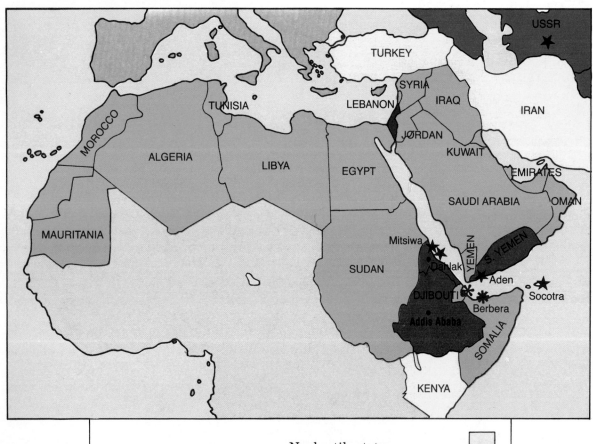

USSR

TURKEY

SYRIA

LEBANON

IRAQ

IRAN

MOROCCO

TUNISIA

JORDAN

KUWAIT

EMIRATES

ALGERIA

LIBYA

EGYPT

SAUDI ARABIA

OMAN

MAURITANIA

Mitsiwa

Dahlak

YEMEN

S. YEMEN

SUDAN

Aden

Socotra

DJIBOUTI

Berbera

Addis Ababa

SOMALIA

KENYA

| | | |
|---|---|---|
| Soviet military bases | ★ | Nonhostile states |
| French military bases | ✳ | Members of the Arab League |
| US military bases | ✴ | Israel |
| | | Ethiopia, USSR, & allies |

## Ethnic Groups in Ethiopia

While the coastal regions of the Horn were colonized by European powers at the end of the nineteenth century, the Ethiopian state, built on the interior highlands, remained in the hands of Christian Amhara. Taking advantage of inter-European rivalries, Ethiopia succeeded in building up a vast empire which embraced, in the south particularly, non-Christian peoples. The traditional antagonism between Christian Ethiopians and Muslim Somalis was further fueled by the inclusion of the Ogaden, peopled by Somalis, in the empire.

After the overthrow of the Emperor Haile Selassie, who had long been a favored ally of the United States in the region (1974), Ethiopia was radicalized and proclaimed itself Marxist-Leninist.

Confronted by the territorial demands of Somalia (militarily linked by a pact to the USSR), and weakened by civil war, it could win the war in the Ogaden (1977–1978) only with the help of the Soviet about-face toward Somalia and the intervention of Cuban troops.

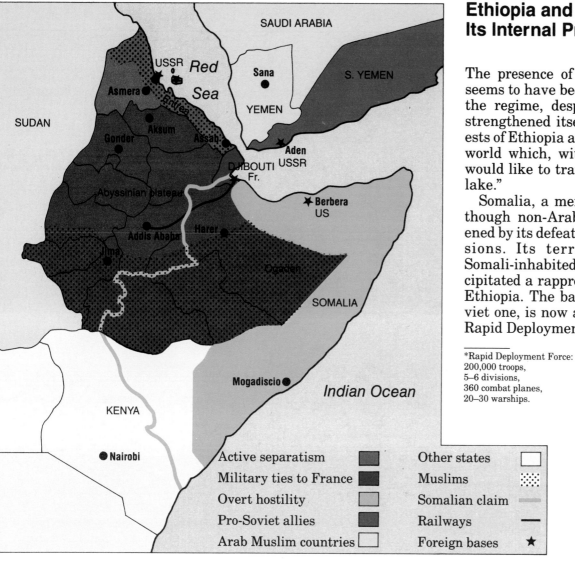

## Ethiopia and Its Internal Problems

The presence of the Soviets and the Cubans seems to have become permanent, even though the regime, despite the war in Eritrea, has strengthened itself. In the Red Sea, the interests of Ethiopia are opposed to those of the Arab world which, with Saudi Arabia in the lead, would like to transform this sea into an "Arab lake."

Somalia, a member of the Arab League (although non-Arab), has been seriously weakened by its defeats, and suffers Ethiopian incursions. Its territorial claims concerning Somali-inhabited regions in Kenya have precipitated a rapprochement between Kenya and Ethiopia. The base at Berbera, formerly a Soviet one, is now an American base open to the Rapid Deployment Force.*

*Rapid Deployment Force:
200,000 troops,
5–6 divisions,
360 combat planes,
20–30 warships.

**Map legend:**

| | |
|---|---|
| Active separatism | |
| Military ties to France | |
| Overt hostility | |
| Pro-Soviet allies | |
| Arab Muslim countries | |
| Other states | |
| Muslims | |
| Somalian claim | |
| Railways | |
| Foreign bases | ★ |

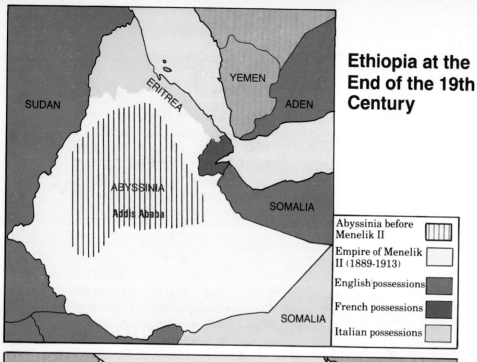

## Ethiopia at the End of the 19th Century

| | |
|---|---|
| Abyssinia before Menelik II | |
| Empire of Menelik II (1889-1913) | |
| English possessions | |
| French possessions | |
| Italian possessions | |

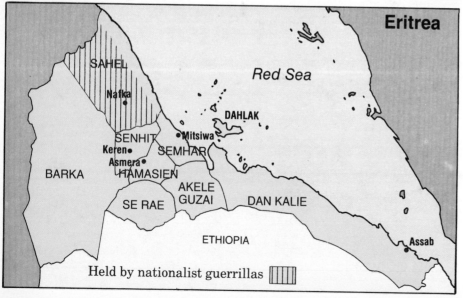

### Eritrea

Held by nationalist guerrillas

## Eritrea

Eritrea was an Italian colony until World War II, then was administered by the British (1941–1952). It did not, like the other Italian colonies, win independence. By a decision of the UN, it was attached to Ethiopia as an autonomous territory (1952). Ten years later, the emperor integrated Eritrea as a province. After 1961, a separatist movement developed, Muslim in origin, but spreading to Christians (each religious group having about half the total population) and supported by the Arab states.

The fall of Haile Selassie did not alter the imperial character of Ethiopia. In spite of Soviet and Cuban aid, the Popular Front for the Liberation of Eritrea (Marxist-Leninist) resisted offensives by Addis Ababa. For Ethiopia, Eritrea represents access to the sea. The USSR has obtained maritime bases in Eritrea. Sudan, formerly openly hostile to Addis Ababa, has to take into account the strengthening of Mengistu's regime and the help given by this regime to the dissidents in southern Sudan (1982).

# China and Its Environment

China is a vast country that is strategically isolated. To the north there is the USSR, with which there is a long-standing territorial dispute. In the era of the unequal treaties (those signed to China's disadvantage by various Western countries have long since been nullified), China ceded to Russia in 1853 2,500,000 sq. km. of territory east of the Ussuri as far as the coastal provinces. Absorbed because of their territorial continuity, these regions (which were not inhabited by Chinese) have remained Soviet, but China laid claim to them from the very beginning of the Sino-Soviet conflict.* There was fighting between Chinese and Russians on the Ussuri (1969). After a decade of Sino-American relations, China, disappointed in its hope of obtaining American help in modernizing its military equipment, is seeking an arrangement with the Soviet Union. A normalization of relations would allow it to attend to pressing domestic and economic problems: agriculture, industry, technology, and modernization of the armed forces.

To the south, China is hostile to Vietnamese hegemony over the Indochinese peninsula and would like to see, both in Vientiane and Phnom Penh, governments hostile to the Vietnamese, whose alliance with Moscow is seen as an encirclement. China's only ally in Southeast Asia is a weakened Pakistan. India, beyond the Himalayan barrier, remains hostile.

Heir to a great civilization that has profoundly influenced its neighbors (Vietnam, Korea, Japan) and conquered a vast empire to the west and north of

China's original eighteen provinces, the People's Republic has the advantage of a homogeneous population (92% are Han Chinese) with exceptional abilities, whose initial enthusiasm was largely eroded by fifteen years of political struggles and economic stagnation, aggravated by bureaucratic inertia. For the time being, the status of Hong Kong, like that of Macao, is useful to China's trade. Taiwan remains a secondary problem. As for foreign policy, especially regarding the Third World, after numerous years marked by setbacks, it is today conducted on more realistic lines. It is essentially by relying on its own organizational and productive abilities that China, by managing its security through a prudent and adaptable policy, can hope to raise itself, with great effort, to the rank of a great power, a rank that no state is anxious to see it attain.

### Cereals*

| | | |
|---|---|---|
| Wheat | 12.5% | (third)† |
| Corn | 11 | (second) |
| Rice | 35 | (first) |
| Barley | 11 | |
| Millet | 36 | (first) |
| Potatoes | 5 | |
| Soy | 16 | (second) |
| Peanuts | 20 | (second) |
| Cotton | 19 | (second) |
| Pork | 41 | (first) |

*18% of world production, based on seven principal grains.
†World rank.

**China under Foreign Influence (1904)**

Mongolian Tuva

Russ. military occup.

Russ. annexations (19th cent.)

Russ. sphere of influence

Japanese sphere of influence

English sphere of influence

Trans-Siberian RR

European concessions

*Underpopulated Mongolia, whose strategic position between China and the USSR is obvious, with its 3,000 km. of frontiers, fears the Chinese, particularly for demographic reasons.

## Major Cereals

Rice ▨
Wheat ▩

## Railways

Railways ——

## Hong Kong

Guangzhou (Canton)

Hong Kong

Kowloon

Victoria

Macao (Port.)

## Industrial China

| | |
|---|---|
| Industrial areas | ▢ |
| Industrial centers | ■ |
| Nuclear power plants | ✪ |
| Iron | ◆ |
| Other ores | ● |
| Oil and natural gas | ▲— |
| Coal | ⬮ |

| Underground Resources | World Production | Reserves |
|---|---|---|
| Coal and lignite | 19 % | 28 % |
| Petroleum | 3 | 3 |
| Iron | 8.3 | 4 |
| Boron | — * | 38 |
| Manganese | 6 | — * |
| Tungsten | 26 | 47 |
| Vanadium | 14 | 13 |
| Antimony | 18 | 39 |

——
*No data.

145

**Manchus**

**Tadjiks**

**Montagnards**

**Distribution of Population**

**1980: 980 Million People**
**2000: 1.2 Billion People**

146

Peoples of China

Han Chinese

Muslim

Tibetan

Mongol

Turkish-speaking

Korean

Thai

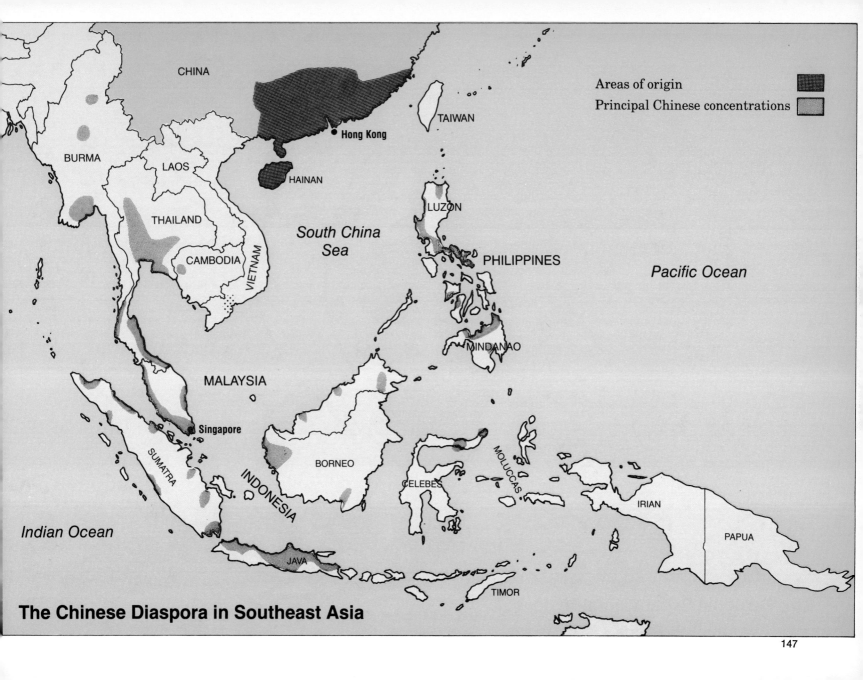

The Chinese Diaspora in Southeast Asia

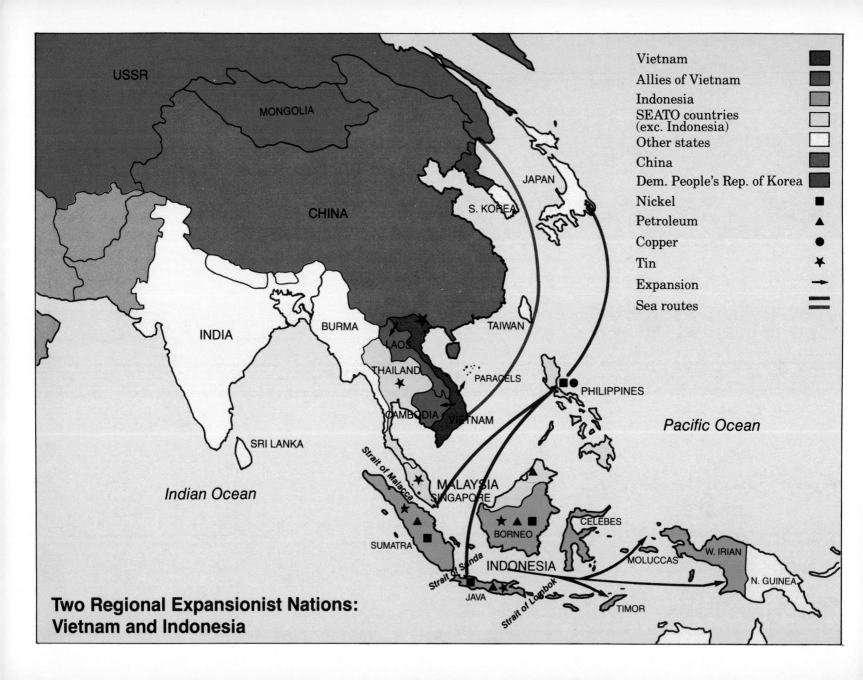

**Two Regional Expansionist Nations: Vietnam and Indonesia**

Legend:

Vietnam
Allies of Vietnam
Indonesia
SEATO countries (exc. Indonesia)
Other states
China
Dem. People's Rep. of Korea
Nickel ■
Petroleum ▲
Copper ●
Tin ★
Expansion →
Sea routes ═

USSR
MONGOLIA
CHINA
JAPAN
S. KOREA
INDIA
BURMA
TAIWAN
LAOS
THAILAND
PARACELS
PHILIPPINES
CAMBODIA
VIETNAM
SRI LANKA
Pacific Ocean
Indian Ocean
Strait of Malacca
MALAYSIA
SINGAPORE
CELEBES
BORNEO
MOLUCCAS
W. IRIAN
SUMATRA
Strait of Sunda
INDONESIA
N. GUINEA
JAVA
Strait of Lombok
TIMOR

# Southeast Asia

Monsoon Asia is predominantly made up of peninsulas and islands surrounded by sea lanes. Like the whole of eastern Asia, it is an area of high agricultural production (rice) and dense population (except Laos). Without ethnic or religious unity (Hinduism, Buddhism, Islam, Confucianism, and Catholicism), Southeast Asia is characterized by societies that are highly structured, with a national consciousness that is often very old and with considerable cultural depth.

The victory of the North Vietnamese in 1975 and the intervention in Cambodia (1978) signified the hegemony of Vietnam over the Indochinese peninsula, provoking the militant hostility of China. This resulted in an armed Sino-Vietnamese confrontation (1979) and in the support given by Thailand and Malaysia (both members of ASEAN*) to the various Khmer forces fighting the Hanoi-backed regime in Cambodia.

The withdrawal of Vietnamese forces, whose military superiority is quite apparent, is out of the question so long as there is no guarantee that Cambodia will be led by a pro-Vietnamese government. Chinese power is perceived as a threat by the Vietnamese, who feel that their hegemony over the Indochinese peninsula gives them a status as a regional power that cannot be ignored.

China in turn feels threatened by the alliance between the USSR and Vietnam. Despite the existence of chronic guerrilla wars (Thailand, Malaysia, Burma, Cambodia, Laos, the Philippines), no existing regime appears threatened by them. Economically, the most dynamic states are Singapore, Thailand, and Malaysia. But it is interesting to note that the two regional powers that have made territorial advances are Vietnam and Indonesia (Moluccas, 1950–1952; New Guinea, 1961–1962; East Timor, 1976–1977); Indonesia also has designs on North Borneo.

*Association of Southeast Asian Nations, founded in 1967. This economic and political organization comprises Indonesia, the Philippines, Singapore, and Thailand.

## Population (in millions)

|  | 1950 | 1980 | 2000 |
|---|---|---|---|
| Indonesia | 77 | 148 | 216 |
| Malaysia | 6.1 | 14 | 21 |
| Philippines | 20 | 49 | 77 |
| Singapore | 1 | 2.4 | 3 |
| Thailand | 20 | 47 | 68 |
| Vietnam | 30 | 55 | 88 |
| Cambodia | 4 | 6.9 | 10 |
| Laos | 2 | 3.4 | 5 |
| Burma | 19 | 35 | 54 |
| Hong Kong | 2 | 5.1 | 6 |
| Taiwan | 8 | 18 | 25 |

## East Asia: One of the Rare Third World Regions with Sustained and Rapid Growth

|  | 1980 | (annual % rate) 1985 (prediction) |
|---|---|---|
| South Korea | 3.5 | 6.0 |
| Hong Kong | 9.0 | 9.6 |
| Indonesia | 9.3 | 9.6 |
| Malaysia | 8.0 | 9.5 |
| Philippines | 5.2 | 8.2 |
| Taiwan | 6.4 | 8.0 |
| Thailand | 6.3 | 8.0 |

## Ethnic Groups

| Vietnamese | |
| --- | --- |
| Chinese | |
| Thai | |
| Khmer | |
| Tibeto-Burman | |
| Karenes | |
| Miao-yao | |
| | — |

## Cambodia (Kampuchea)

| Railways | — |
| --- | --- |
| Khmer rouge | ▲ |
| Son Sann forces | ✳ |
| Sihanouk forces | ★ |

## An Area of Geopolitical Fluidity

On the borders of China and several Southeast Asian countries, the profusion of minorities, their overlapping, and the fact that they are geographically exclusive makes the geopolitical situation particularly fluid. Political guerrillas that are more or less manipulated by one power or another (China, USA, etc.) and bands of irregulars engaging in the opium trade continue to find rear bases or sanctuaries in these areas.

**Kashmir**

Claimed by China ▦

Claimed by Pakistan ☐

Armed conflicts ★

Muslims ▥

Himalayan barrier ▨

AFGHANISTAN

PAKISTAN

KASHMIR

India-China 1959-1960

India-Pakistan 1965

CHINA

Delhi

NEPAL

India-China 1959-1960

India-China 1962

BHUTAN

ASSAM

India-Pakistan 1965

India-Pakistan 1971

BANGLA DESH

Calcutta

BURMA

Bombay

Goa

ANDAMAN IS.

Madras

Pondicherry

Trivandrum

SRI LANKA

NICOBAR IS.

# India: Its Security Perception

India is, with China, the only great regional power in Asia. India, a quasi-industrial power that belongs to the nuclear club (1974), has more to fear from its internal disparities and distortions, fueled by an almost uncontrollable population growth, than from its neighbors.

India is not a nation, but a civilization. Since independence, the language of administration has been English. In addition to its linguistic and ethnic divisions (especially north–south), there is the problem of its very large Muslim minority (almost 20%). Social cleavages, partly rigidified by the caste system, exclude 105 million Harijans (formerly Untouchables), despite legislation.

Twice defeated by China (1959, 1962), India has grown stronger since, and China seems unlikely in the foreseeable future to embark on incursions that, in any case, would be logistically difficult to make on a large scale.

Pakistan, which claims Muslim-inhabited Kashmir, is today, after many conflicts, greatly weakened by its defeat in Bangladesh by Indian troops and by the closeness, on the Afghan frontier, of Soviet troops. India has always had excellent relations with the USSR (especially in the matter of military supplies) while remaining a model of nonalignment. However, the excessive proximity of Soviet troops might worry a political elite that is skillful and conscious of its interests.

The overseas Indian population is numerous throughout eastern Africa, from Kenya to South Africa, as well as in the eastern part of the Indian Ocean (Malaysia, Singapore, etc.). India is one of the few Third World countries to have the means to carry out its south–south industrial projects. Given its ambitions in the Indian Ocean area, it would seem that strengthening its maritime capabilities, which are already quite considerable, is necessary.

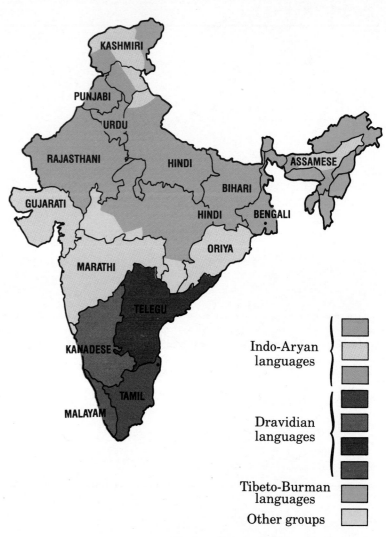

Indo-Aryan languages

Dravidian languages

Tibeto-Burman languages

Other groups

**Main Linguistic Groups**

# Economic India

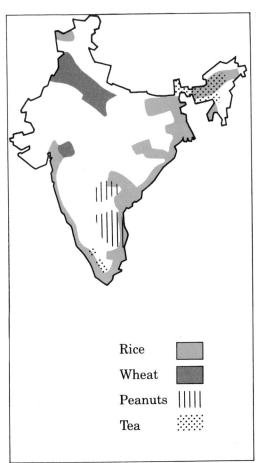

**MAIN AGRICULTURAL RESOURCES**

Rice

Wheat

Peanuts ||||

Tea

**INDUSTRY**

Industrial regions

Major railways

Petroleum ▲

Bauxite ■

Coal ●

Iron ◆

**Cereals—9% of world production, on the basis of principal cereals**

| | |
|---|---|
| Rice | 20% |
| Wheat | 7% |
| Millet | 30% |
| Cassava | 6% |
| Sugar | 5% |
| Potatoes | 4% |
| Peanuts | 34% |
| Cotton | 10% |

## Mineral and Energy Resources

| | World Production (%) | |
|---|---|---|
| Coal | 3% | |
| Iron ore | 5% | (5.5% of reserves) |
| Manganese | 6% | |
| Ilmenite (titanium) | 20% | (reserves) |
| Thorium | 30% | (reserves) |

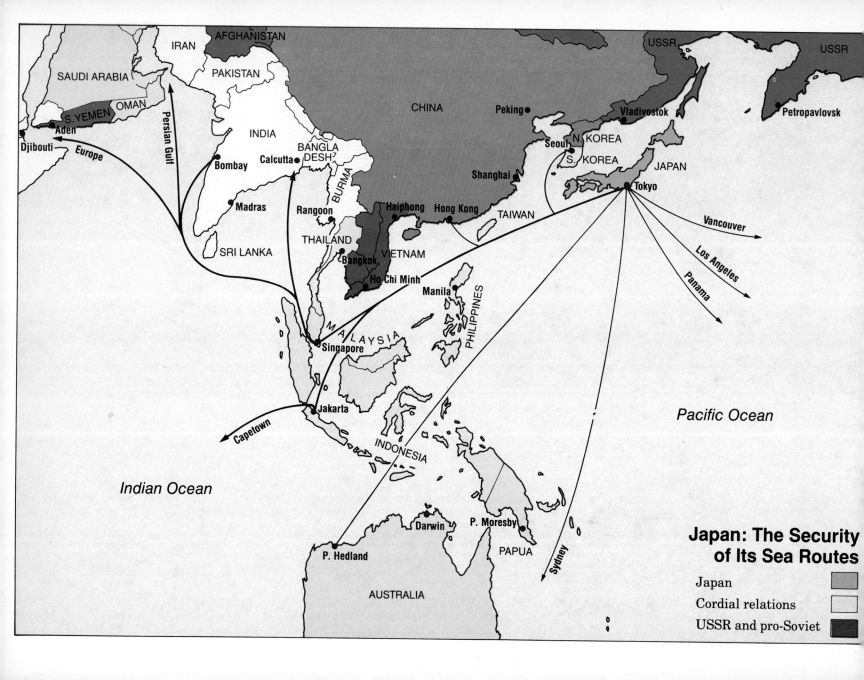

IRAN
AFGHANISTAN
SAUDI ARABIA
PAKISTAN
S. YEMEN OMAN
Aden
Djibouti    Europe
Persian Gulf
INDIA
BANGLA DESH
Bombay    Calcutta
BURMA
Madras
Rangoon
SRI LANKA
THAILAND
Bangkok
Ho Chi Minh
VIETNAM
Haiphong    Hong Kong
TAIWAN
Shanghai
Peking
CHINA
USSR
Vladivostok
USSR
Petropavlovsk
Seoul    N. KOREA
S. KOREA
JAPAN
Tokyo
Vancouver
Los Angeles
Panama
MALAYSIA
Singapore
Manila
PHILIPPINES
Jakarta
Capetown
INDONESIA

*Indian Ocean*

*Pacific Ocean*

Darwin    P. Moresby
P. Hedland    PAPUA
Sydney

AUSTRALIA

# Japan: The Security of Its Sea Routes

Japan
Cordial relations
USSR and pro-Soviet

Most active areas
Other areas
Coal
Petroleum ▲
Hydroelectricity ●

HOKKAIDO
Sapporo
Tomakomai
Hachinohe
Akita
Yamagata
Fukushima
Kashima
HONSHU
Tokyo
Yokohama
Nagoya
Kobe
Hiroshima
Kita-Kyushu
Osaka
SHIKOKU
KYUSHU
Kagoshima

Imports

| Coal | Oil & natural gas | Minerals |
|------|-------------------|----------|
| 77% | 98% | about 90% |
| Australia | Persian Gulf | Australia |
| N. America | Indonesia | South Africa |
| India | etc. | Southern Asia |
| etc. | | Brazil |
| | | etc. |

# Japan: An Industrial Power

Japan is the only Afro-Asian country that succeeded in responding to the Western challenge and in carrying out an industrial revolution launched in 1868. Since then, it has spared no effort to maintain its independence. At the end of a war in which it had imposed its harsh law on East Asia, Japan suffered nuclear tragedy (Hiroshima, Nagasaki).

Provided with democratic institutions during the American occupation, demilitarized* Japan reoriented its energy, organizational abilities, cohesion (founded, among other things, on a population whose homogeneity has been carefully preserved), and social discipline toward economic and commercial goals. Lacking resources, and aided by a dynamism backed by modern business organization and the consensus of wage earners, Japan has succeeded, in three decades, in outclassing almost all the industrial countries, becoming an irresistible competitor. Militarily, Japan is highly vulnerable, but its economic vulnerability is even greater, given the country's heavy dependence on the world market: A break in supplies of raw materials from the Third World or the erection of barriers in the industrial countries where it sells its products, would be serious. Japan's competitiveness tends to provoke protectionist measures in some countries. Japan's security, at the present time, rests on the continuation, as far as it can be done, of free trade.

*Japan is linked militarily to the United States.

Having succeeded in controlling its birth rate in the 1950s, enjoying a productive agriculture, engaging in large-scale fishing, and endowed with a hard-working and docile population, Japan has the necessary determination to face all challenges. Its lines of communication—which are vital, especially from the Gulf—are guaranteed by a large merchant fleet. In the framework of new rules of the game to which it has adapted, Japan seems to have realized many of the objectives it had during the years of empire.

## Population Density

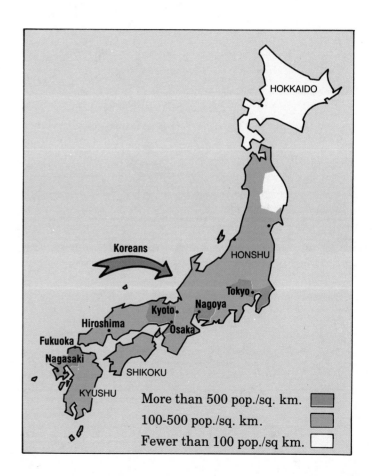

## Urbanized Zones in the South

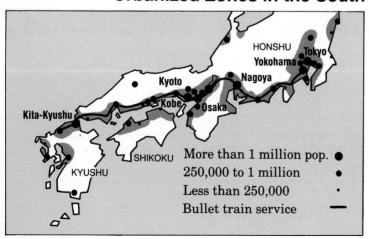

More than 1 million pop. ●
250,000 to 1 million ●
Less than 250,000 ·
Bullet train service —

More than 500 pop./sq. km. ▨
100-500 pop./sq. km. ▨
Fewer than 100 pop./sq km. ☐

## Industrial Power: % of World Production

**Production**

| | |
|---|---|
| Steel | 14.0 |
| Copper | 11.5 |
| Aluminum | 7.0 |
| Shipbuilding | 54.0 |
| Autos | 24.5 |
| Commercial vehicles | 42.0 |
| Resins and plastics (petrochemicals) | 14.0 |
| Synthetic rubber | 11.0 |
| Synthetic fabrics | 13.0 |

## Resources

**Foodstuffs**

| | |
|---|---|
| Rice | approx. 13 million tons |
| Fish | 15% (of world total) |

**Fuels—Ores**

| | |
|---|---|
| Coal | 12% of total consumed |
| Hydroelectricity | 13% of total electricity consumed |

## Imports (Dependencies)

| | |
|---|---|
| Wheat, cereals, agric. products | 25% of needs |
| Copper | 100% of needs |
| Coal | 88% of needs |
| Oil | 99% of needs |
| Uranium | 100% of needs |
| Iron | 92% of needs |
| Other ores | +90% (except lead, zinc, silver) |

## Japanese Foreign Trade 1981 (%)

| Exports | | Imports |
|---|---|---|
| 25 | United States | 18 |
| 16 | Western Europe | 8 |
| 13 | EEC | 6 |
| 15 | OPEC | 38 |
| 20 | Far East | 17 |
| 24 | Others | 19 |
| $152 | Total value (billions of dollars) | $143 |

# Australia

Australia cooperates militarily with the United States in ANZUS (Australia, New Zealand, United States) as well as with Singapore and Malaysia in the framework of the five-nation agreement (Great Britain, Australia, New Zealand, Singapore, Malaysia). It participates in the sea, air, and naval forces detached by the American Seventh Fleet in the Indian Ocean.

Australia occupies an exceptional geostrategic position between the Indian Ocean and the Pacific. As the largest state in the Pacific, it seeks to play a role as a regional power. Its mineral resources are considerable: It has offshore oil; in addition, it is a leading world exporter of grain and cereals.

A close trading partner of Japan, to which it supplies many raw materials, Australia seeks to work with New Zealand, which plays a more modest role.

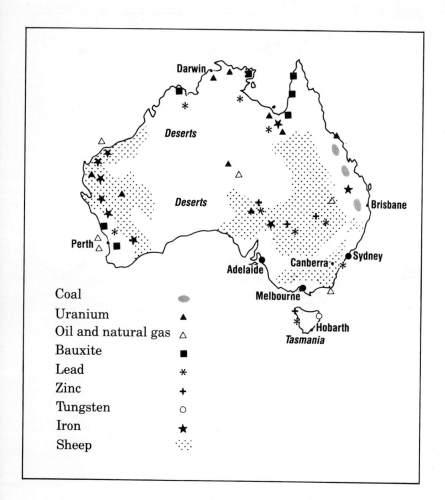

| Sheep | 12% (world flocks) 2nd rank | |
| --- | --- | --- |
| Uranium | 3.5% world prod. | 7% reserves |
| Iron | 10.5% | 11% |
| Manganese | 7.5% | 6% |
| Tungsten | 6.0% | 4% |
| Cobalt | 6.0% | 11% |
| Bauxite | 28.5% | 20% |
| Lead | 11.5% | 14% |
| Zinc | 8.5% | 10% |

Coal

Uranium ▲

Oil and natural gas △

Bauxite ■

Lead *

Zinc +

Tungsten ○

Iron ★

Sheep

# Australia: Perception of Its Security

Australia's traditional sensitivity to possible threats from Asia is fueled by awareness of its isolation in the southern hemisphere and its low population.

USA

CANADA

San Francisco
6450 naut. miles

USSR

MONGOLIA

CHINA

KOREA

JAPAN

INDIA

TAIWAN

THAILAND

PHILIPPINES

VIETNAM

SS-20

MALAYSIA

HAWAII

Pacific Ocean

ASEAN   INDONESIA

Darwin

TU-95

Indian Ocean

AUSTRALIA

Brisbane

Perth

Sydney

Melbourne

Auckland

NEW ZEALAND

| | |
|---|---|
| USA and allies | |
| Good relations | |
| USSR and allies | |
| China | |
| Toward the USA | |
| SS 20 (range) | |
| TU 95 (range) | |
| Soviet bases | ★ |

159

# Latin America

Latin America is economically dominated by the United States, to which it is linked by the Treaty of Rio (1947), an inter-American mutual defense treaty, and by the Organization of American States (1948), from which Cuba was excluded in 1962 at the time of the missile crisis.

The United States historically has defended its geostrategic area: Guatemala (1954), Bay of Pigs (1961), and, following Cuba's move to the left, through the Alliance for Progress, a combination of economic assistance and training of Latin American counterguerrilla forces. (All the Latin American guerrilla movements of the 1960s have been defeated: Brazil [coup d'état, 1964]; intervention in the Dominican Republic [1965]; destabilization and fall of the Allende government in Chile [1973].)

Basically, the Latin American world is more stable than it appears: In three decades, there have been only two radical political changes—Cuba (1959) and Nicaragua (1979).

Latin America has seen exceptionally rapid population growth: 132 million in 1945; 303 million in 1975; 600 million projected for 2000. The dominance of the Spanish language (except in Brazil) throughout Latin America should not lead one to overlook the existence of large In-

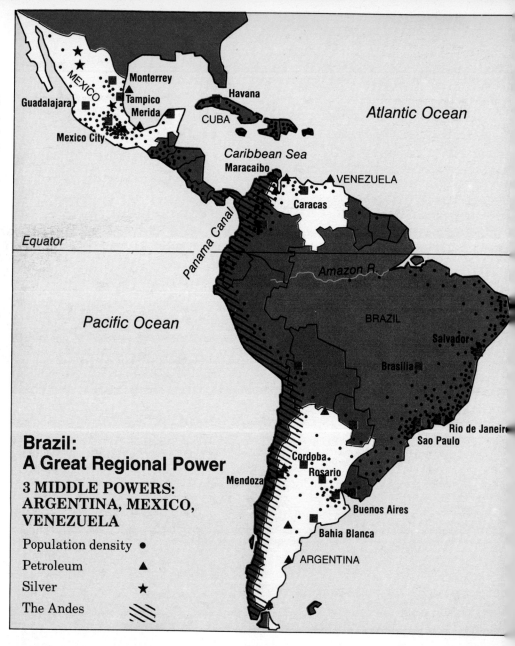

**Brazil:
A Great Regional Power**

**3 MIDDLE POWERS:
ARGENTINA, MEXICO,
VENEZUELA**

Population density •

Petroleum ▲

Silver ★

The Andes ⧄

dian populations (Bolivia, Peru, Ecuador, Guatemala, Honduras, Mexico, etc.), almost all of whom are marginal people in their societies. Outside Brazil, the black or colored populations are concentrated in the Caribbean basin.

There has been no integration or resolution of the crisis-laden social distortions, despite strong nationalist feelings and social problems to which the Catholic Church has given expression. Catholicism is a force to be reckoned with; at the end of the century, the majority of Catholics in the world will be Latin Americans.

The continent has substantial resources, although only one country is in a position to export a surplus in agriculture or livestock (Argentina), and only one has really large mineral resources (Brazil). Oil, in modest quantities, is exploited in Mexico, Venezuela, and Ecuador. Peru has five major minerals, but Chile (copper), Bolivia (tin), and Jamaica (bauxite) have only one each. Although backward areas, notably among the Andean countries and in Central America, would seem to have limited prospects, Latin America as a whole is in a much better situation than most of Asia and Africa.

The present crisis and the wars in Central America are perceived by the United States as a test of political will, and it seems that everything will be done to ensure that the Pax Americana prevails in the end.

Three decades ago, Argentina seemed, given its cultural level and its agricultural and cattle wealth, to be destined to become a major power. But neither in terms of development, population, or institutions has Argentina lived up to its promise. The failure of the Falklands gamble, underestimating the capacity of Mrs. Thatcher's government to respond, has accentuated the crisis in Argentine society. The relations of convenience between right-wing soldiers and the USSR since 1980, based on common interests, is viewed with annoyance in Washington, which was obliged to support Great Britain during the Falklands crisis.

Venezuela, with a small population, can lay claim to the role of middling regional power only because of its oil. Its geostrategic position is linked to the Caribbean as a whole, and its interest lies in maintaining stability there. The 200-nautical-mile limit would allow Venezuela to exercise rights over a significant part of the Caribbean. The drawing of the limits of the continental shelf raises problems with its rival Colombia, which exports a large part of its work force to Venezuela.

Mexico, once considered a rising regional power, demonstrated its fragility in 1982 with the collapse of its currency. Contrary to what it has been claiming for several decades, the Institutional Revolutionary Party (PRI), which has been in power for half a century, has not succeeded in modernizing the country's institutions. Corruption, which is typical of the system, has increased with the oil boom. Today, Mexico is faced with a crisis that may well have serious social consequences.

# Brazil: South–South Perception

The Organization of American States (OAS), formed in 1948, reaffirmed the cooperation among the American nations (the First Congress of American States, 1889), as did the reciprocal-aid Treaty of Rio, signed in 1947. Members include: All the South American states except British and French Guyana; the Antilles, except for Cuba, which has not participated, including Jamaica, Haiti, the Dominican Republic, Antigua and Barbuda, Dominique, St. Lucia, St. Vincent and the Grenadines, Trinidad, and Tobago. Different economic alliances regroup some of these countries, such as the Andean group, countries of the Caribbean basin, and the Association for Latin American Integration (ALADI).

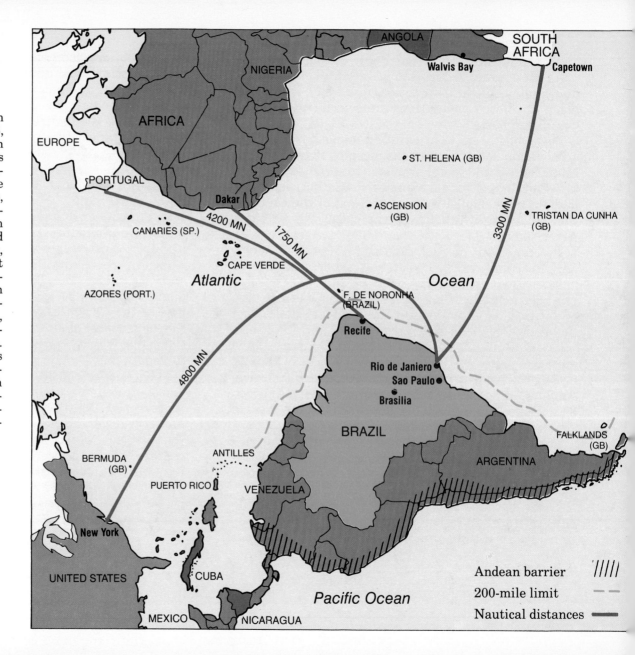

# Brazil: Occupation of the Land

| Corn | 6% |
|---|---|
| Cassava | 30% |
| Soya | 17% |
| Sugar | 10% |
| Beef | 7% |
| Pork | 5% |

Developed area

Indians

Major railways

New highways

Roads under construction

Waterways

More than 5 million pop. ◯
More than 1 million pop. ◯
More than 500,000 pop. ○
More than 100,000 pop. •
< 500,000 pop. ·

| | | |
|---|---|---|
| Hydroelectricity | 6% (world prod.) | |
| Iron | 11.5% (world prod.) | 20% res. |
| Manganese | 8% (world prod.) | |
| Niobium | 87% (world prod.) | 23% res. |
| Bauxite | 5% (world prod.) | 10.5% res. |
| Rutile | | 74% res. |
| Thorium | | 6% res. |
| Tantalum | 25.5% (world prod.) | |

## The Brazilian Terrain

Equatorial & tropical forests

Tropical cultivation

Caatinga (brush)

Savannas

Prairie/coniferous forests

# Brazil and Its Resources

Brazil, whose perception of the world is south–south oriented, is like a promontory at the eastern tip of the South American continent, less than 3,000 km from Dakar. It is the only Portuguese-speaking state in Latin America; it is also the most populous and is the only regional power. Moreover, it has considerable ambitions, but the economic base that would enable them to be realized is still lacking.

The development of Brazil depends on the conquest and control of its own territory and its ability, which is currently uncertain, to maintain dynamic growth.

But whatever the difficulties, Brazil is lucky to be able to count on a vast quantity of unexploited resources and is better placed than others to pursue a go-ahead policy.

A multiracial society based on "cordial domination" and mixing may, despite appearances, be the scene of racial problems that are also social problems.

Once tempted to base its African policy on South Africa, Brazil has reoriented its relations toward the Portuguese-speaking states and Nigeria. The creation of a navy suited to its ambitions should be a priority.

Intensive agriculture

Extensive agriculture

Coal

Hydroelectricity

Petroleum

Nickel

Iron

Manganese

Copper

Nuclear power plants

Hydroelectric systems

Refineries

Storage facilities

Electric networks

Pipelines

**THE INDUSTRIALIZED CENTER**

# Brazil and Its Geopolitical Aspirations

*Portugal and its colonies occupy an enviable situation in the world beyond Latin America that can never be adequately stressed. In both the North Atlantic, where the Azores, Madeira, and Cape Verde constitute unparalleled defensive outposts, and in the south of Africa, where Angola and Mozambique almost mark out a Lusitanian equator right opposite the main power center that we in Brazil represent, and that is without mentioning Guinea, a second Dakar. . . .\**

*By its prominent situation in the nearest semicircle, which is vital for South America and Brazil's security, this area creates a Portuguese responsibility that we must be ready to take on at any moment.*

*The Latin world, in its turn, though its ties are looser, must consciously accept a sphere of solidarities that has come to include a large part of the European peninsula and almost the whole of West Africa. And this is because we are a Latin country, by our origin and by our culture, with an outstanding and hardworking population.*

(Golbery do Couto e Silva, *Conjuntura politica nacional o poder executivo e geopolitico do Brasil,* Livraria José Olympio editore, Rio, 1981, p. 195; from the French translation by Alain Mangin.)

———
\*Written in 1959.

# Central America: Zone of Conflicts

Central America, divided into a group of micro-states, is a geographical area traditionally controlled by the United States, which has intervened on numerous occasions from 1903 (Panama) to 1965 (Dominican Republic). Central America is currently an arena of East–West confrontations arising out of local conflicts.

The situations in Nicaragua, El Salvador, Guatemala, and Honduras are interdependent. The United States is aiding El Salvador and Guatemala in their fights against insurrections and is using Honduras as a base, particularly to shore up the anti-Sandinista movements in Nicaragua.

Nicaragua, allied to the Cubans and the Soviets, is assisting the guerrillas in El Salvador. The armed struggles in Guatemala (in which Indians are taking part) and in El Salvador, Marxist in inspiration, are well organized. But the United States cannot accept their successes and the spread of revolutionary movements in the region.

The zones held by the Salvadoran guerrilla movement, Morazan and Chalatenango, are poor and quite densely populated, despite the exodus caused by the war. The country is increasingly cut in two, but it does not seem likely that either side can win a military victory.

Guatemala, richer and more populous, is having to face an insurrection in which a large Indian population is taking part. This fact is perhaps the major new feature of the decade.

## Panama: The Canal Zone

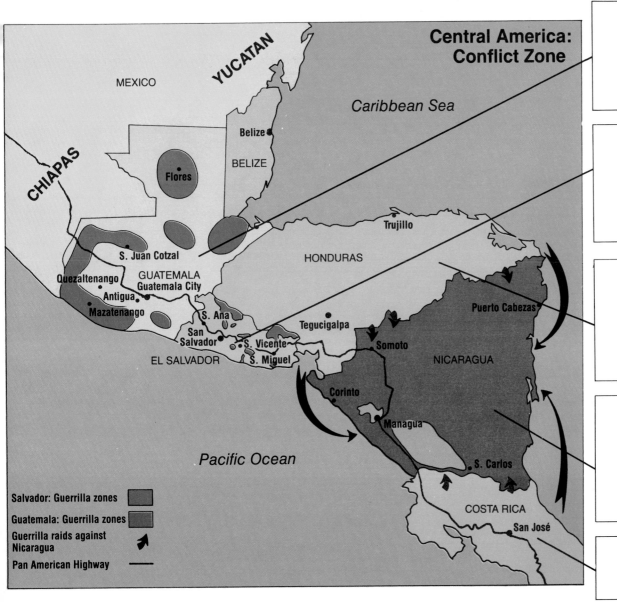

**Central America:
Conflict Zone**

MEXICO

YUCATAN

CHIAPAS

*Caribbean Sea*

Belize

BELIZE

Flores

Trujillo

S. Juan Cotzal

HONDURAS

Quezaltenango

GUATEMALA

Guatemala City

Puerto Cabezas

Antigua

Mazatenango

S. Ana

Tegucigalpa

Somoto

San
Salvador

S. Vicente

EL SALVADOR

S. Miguel

NICARAGUA

Corinto

Managua

*Pacific Ocean*

S. Carlos

COSTA RICA

San José

Salvador: Guerrilla zones

Guatemala: Guerrilla zones

Guerrilla raids against
Nicaragua

Pan American Highway

**Guatemala**
109,000 sq. km.; pop. 7 million
Indians: 55 to 60% of population
Urban population: 30%
Security forces: 45,000 men
Army: 23,000 men
Guerrillas: 4,000 to 6,000 men

**El Salvador**
21,000 sq. km.; pop. 4.5 million
Indians: 55 to 60% of population
Urban population: 40%
Security forces: 25,000 men
Army: 16,000 men
Guerrillas: 5,000 to 7,000 men
American advisors: 55

**Honduras**
112,000 sq. km.; pop. 3.7 million
Indians: 30 to 35% of population
Urban population: 35%
Security forces: 25,000 men
Army: 15,000 men
American advisors: 120
Guerrillas: several hundred

**Nicaragua**
130,000 sq. km.; pop. 2.6 million
Indians: 5 to 10% of population
Urban population: 57%
Security forces: 16,000 men
Army: 25,000 men
Soviet or Cuban advisors: 2,000
Anti-Sandinista commandos: 8,000
to 9,000 men

**Costa Rica**
51,000 sq. km.
Population: 2.2 million
Urban population: 46%

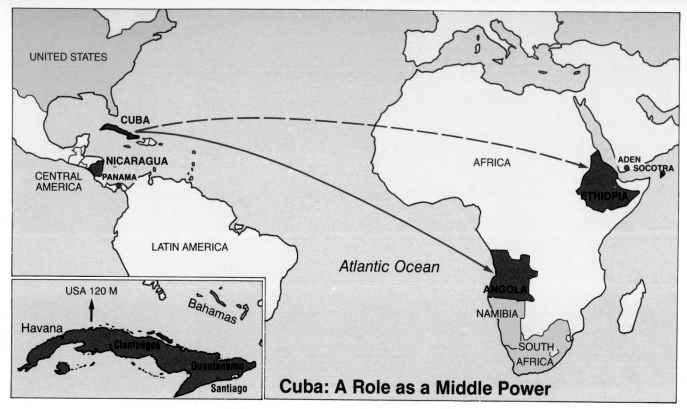

**Cuba: A Role as a Middle Power**

**Despite its small size, Cuba acts as a middle power, but this role is heavily dependent on Soviet logistical support.**

Even though the Cuban presence exists in a reduced form in a number of African states, it directly influences the political situation only in Angola and Ethiopia as a result of the massive intervention of Cuban troops in 1975 and 1977.

For a nation of some 10 million inhabitants, Cuba has, with about 25,000 soldiers, proportionately a very high presence in Africa (for the USA, it would equal nearly 600,000 men).

After its setbacks in Latin America in the 1960s, Cuba has regained an active role there with the Sandinista government in Nicaragua and now has influence over the conflicts in Central America (El Salvador, Guatemala).

**Significant Cuban Presence:**

Angola:          12,000–18,000
Ethiopia:          7,000–9,000
Other African countries: More than 3,000, including 1,000 in Mozambique and 800 in the Congo.

# NATURAL CONSTRAINTS

Natural constraints determine the density of human settlement and the eventual exploitation or development of mineral or agricultural resources. They may be obstacles or advantages in times of war and guerrilla activity. Nature, as a constraint and as a resource, is an element of strategy.

# Basic Data

**World Land Use (%)**

| | Cultivated Land | Pasture | Forest | Uncultivated Land |
|---|---|---|---|---|
| USSR | 10% | 17% | 41% | 32% |
| N. America | 14% | 13% | 34% | 39% |
| S. America | 7% | 26% | 51% | 16% |
| Africa | 8% | 30% | 23% | 39% |
| Middle East | 7% | 16% | 12% | 65% |
| Asia (exc. USSR & Middle East) | 33% | 4% | 40% | 23% |
| Europe (exc. USSR) | 26% | 19% | 33% | 22% |
| Oceania | 6% | 60% | 18% | 16% |

**Forests (in millions of hectares)**

| Surfaces Covered | 1978 | 2000 |
|---|---|---|
| USSR | 785 | 775 |
| North America | 470 | 464 |
| South America | 550 | 329 |
| Africa | 188 | 150 |
| Asia (except USSR) | 361 | 181 |
| Europe (except USSR) | 140 | 150 |
| Japan | | |
| New Zealand | | |
| Australia | 69 | 68 |
| Total | 2,563 | 2,117 |

# Hot Deserts, Frozen Deserts

Frozen deserts

Hot deserts

Deserts with cold winters

Mountainous deserts

Northern forests

Dense forests

Savannas

## Major Forests and Savannas

# Constraints of Topography

- Low mountains
- Middle-size mountains
- High mountains

**Rainfall and Snow**

- Snowbound areas
- Heavy snow
- Rainfall (+ 2000 mm)
- Rainfall (1500-2000 mm)
- Rainfall (1000-1500 mm)

# Availability of Drinking Water

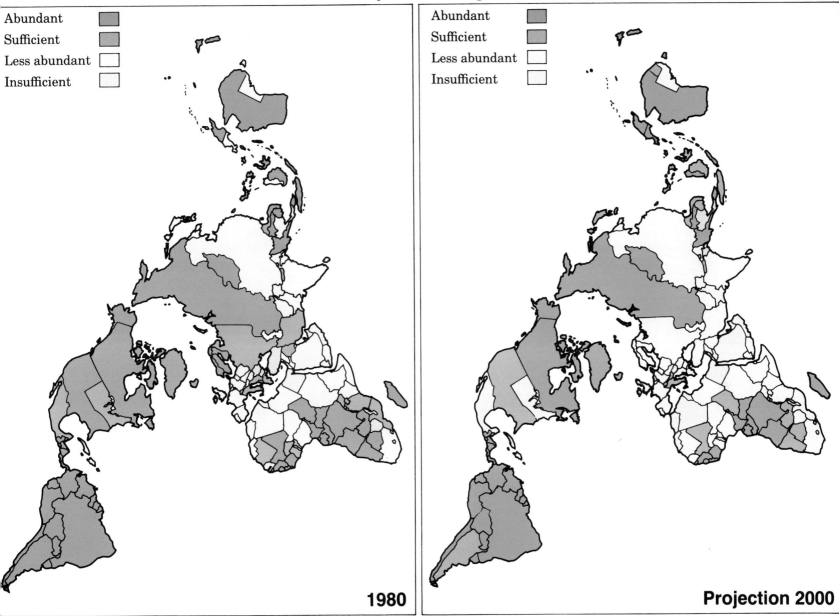

Abundant
Sufficient
Less abundant
Insufficient

Abundant
Sufficient
Less abundant
Insufficient

**1980**

**Projection 2000**

Source: *The Global 2000 Report to the President,* Washington, DC, 1980.

# ECONOMIC DATA

# Rich and Poor in Minerals

The main areas of mineral production and most known reserves are situated in the great industrial states of the northern hemisphere, in South Africa, and in Australia. Western Europe and Japan have few of them.

**Gold production**
South Africa   51%
USSR   31.5%
Canada   3%

Mineral products equal more than 5% of world total.

More than 6 minerals

Poorly supplied

More than 2 minerals

Poorly supplied

DEVELOPED STATES

THIRD WORLD STATES

# Minerals and the Major Producers (% of world total)

| P: production<br>R: reserves | Iron | | Cobalt | | Chrome | | Manganese | | Molybdenum | | Nickel | | Tungsten | | Vanadium | | Bauxite | |
|---|---|---|---|---|---|---|---|---|---|---|---|---|---|---|---|---|---|---|
| | P | R | P | R | P | R | P | R | P | R | P | R | P | R | P | R | P | R |
| **Major producers** | | | | | | | | | | | | | | | | | | |
| South Africa | | | | | 34 | 67 | 23 | 41 | | | | | | | 30.5 | 42 | | |
| Australia | 10.5 | 11 | 6 | 11 | | | 7.5 | 6 | | | | | 6 | | | | 28.5 | 21 |
| Canada | 5.5 | 8.5 | | | | | | | 10.5 | 7 | 26.5 | 15 | | 15 | | | | |
| United States | 8.5 | 5 | | | | | | | 65 | 54 | | | 6 | 8 | 13,5 | | | |
| USSR/Eastern countries | 28 | 30 | 13 | 13 | 37.5 | ? | 39 | 44 | 11 | 9 | 24 | 14 | 17 | 7.5 | 30.5 | 39 | 5.5 | |
| **Important Producers** | | | | | | | | | | | | | | | | | | |
| Bolivia | | | | | | | | | | | | | | | | | | |
| Brazil | 11.5 | 20 | | | | | 8 | | | | | | 6 | | | | | |
| Chile | | | | | | | | | 11 | 25 | | | | | | | 5 | 11 |
| China | 8 | | | | | | 6 | | | | | | | | | | | |
| India | 5.5 | 5.5 | | | | | 6 | | | | | | 26 | 47 | 14 | 13 | | |
| Mexico | | | | | | | 6 | | | | | | | | | | | |
| Peru | | | | | | | | | | | | | | | | | | |
| Zaire | | | 51 | 38 | | | | | | | | | | | | | | |
| **Other producers** | | | | | | | | | | | | | | | | | | |
| Algeria | | | | | | | | | | | | | | | | | | |
| Botswana | | | 5 | | | | | | | | | | | | | | | |
| Cuba | | | | | | | | | | | | | | | | | | |
| Spain | | | | | | | | | | | 5.5 | 5.5 | | | | | | |
| Finland | | | | | | | | | | | | | | | | | | |
| Gabon | | | | | | | 6 | | | | | | | | 7 | | | |
| Guinea | | | | | | | | | | | | | | | | | | |
| Indonesia | | | | | | | | | | | | | | | | | 16 | 26 |
| Jamaica | | | | | | | | | | | | | | | | | | |
| Malaysia | | | | | | | | | | | | | | | | | 14 | 9 |
| Norway | | | | | | | | | | | | | | | | | | |
| N. Caledonia (Fr.) | | | | | | | | | | | | | | | | | | |
| Philippines | | | | | | | | | | | 7 | 25 | | | | | | |
| Thailand | | | | | 6 | | | | | | | | | | | | | |
| Zambia | | | 9 | 12 | | | | | | | | | | | | | | |
| Zimbabwe | | | | | 6 | 30 | | | | | | | | | | | | |
| Total (%)<br>prod. and world reserves | 77.5 | 80 | 84 | 74 | 83.5 | 97 | 95.5 | 91 | 97.5 | 95 | 63 | 64.5 | 61 | 77.5 | 81.5 | 94 | 69 | 67 |

**Notes :**
- Only production and reserves over 5% of the world total are counted.
- ? Indicates probable important production or reserves (lack of data, principally USSR and China).

| P: production / R: reserves | Copper | | Tin | | Lead | | Zinc | | Silver | | Platinum | | Antimony | | Mercury | | Titanium | |
|---|---|---|---|---|---|---|---|---|---|---|---|---|---|---|---|---|---|---|
| | P | R | P | R | P | R | P | R | P | R | P | R | P | R | P | R | R | R |
| **Major producers** | | | | | | | | | | | | | | | | | | |
| South Africa | | | | | | | | | | | 45 | 81 | 16 | 7 | | | 15 | 5 |
| Australia | | | | | 11.5 | 14 | 8.5 | 10 | | | | | | | | | 7 | 7 |
| Canada | 9 | 7 | | | 10.5 | 13 | 17 | 26 | 10.5 | 19 | 5 | | | | | | 25 | |
| United States | 19.5 | 18 | | | 13 | 27 | | 20 | 10.5 | 21 | | | | | 14.5 | 7 | 6 | |
| USSR/Eastern countries | 12 | 7 | 15 | 10 | 17 | 11 | 17 | 9 | 14.5 | 30 | 48 | 16 | 12 | 20 | 32.5 | 11 | ? | ? |
| **Important Producers** | | | | | | | | | | | | | | | | | | |
| Bolivia | | | 10 | | | | | | | | | | 23.5 | 8 | | | | |
| Brazil | | | | | | | | | | | | | | | | | | 74 |
| Chile | 13.5 | 19 | | | | | | | | | | | | | | | | |
| China | | | | 15 | | | | | | | | | 18 | 39 | | ? | | |
| India | | | | | | | | | | | | | | | | | 20 | |
| Mexico | | | | | | | 5.5 | | 14 | 13 | | | | | | | | |
| Peru | | 6 | | | 6 | | 8.5 | | 13 | | | | | | | | | |
| Zaire | 6 | | | | | | | | | | | | | | | | | |
| **Other producers** | | | | | | | | | | | | | | | | | | |
| Algeria | | | | | | | | | | | | | | | 15 | 8 | | |
| Botswana | | | | | | | | | | | | | | | | | | |
| Cuba | | | | | | | | | | | | | | | | | | |
| Spain | | | | | | | | | | | | | | | 15 | 33 | | |
| Finland | | | | | | | | | | | | | | | | | | |
| Gabon | | | | | | | | | | | | | | | | | | |
| Guinea | | | | | | | | | | | | | | | | | | |
| Indonesia | | | 13 | 16 | | | | | | | | | | | | | | |
| Jamaica | | | | | | | | | | | | | | | | | | |
| Malaysia | | | 25 | 12 | | | | | | | | | | | | | | |
| Norway | | | | | | | | | | | | | | | | | 21 | |
| N. Caledonia (Fr.) | | | | | | | | | | | | | | | | | | |
| Philippines | | | | | | | | | | | | | | | | | | |
| Thailand | | | 14 | 12 | | | | | | | | | | | | | | |
| Zambia | 7.5 | 6 | | | | | | | | | | | | | | | | |
| Zimbabwe | | | | | | | | | | | | | | | | | | |
| Total (%) prod. and world reserves | 67.5 | 63 | 77 | 65 | 58 | 65 | 56.5 | 65 | 62.5 | 83 | 98 | 97 | 69.5 | 74 | 77 | 59 | 94 | 86 |

(Titanium reserve columns: Ilmenite | Rutile)

• A number of useful minerals (boron, lithium, magnesium, niobium, strontium, tantalum, thorium) have been left out of this table for lack of data

• Minerals used for fertilizer (potassium, phosphates, etc.) are not included here.

• Titanium: derived primarily from two ores, ilmenite and rutile (incomplete data).

*Source:* U.S. Bureau of Mines.

# Energy and Mineral Resources in the Oceans

Offshore mineral deposits such as deep-sea oil fields are always associated with the continental shelf. Gradually, technological developments are making it possible to operate at greater and greater depths. The number of fields being exploited has increased enormously in the last fifteen years (from 70 in 1965 to over 400 in 1980).

Since 1950, oceanographic research has revealed the mineral riches of the deep sea, which are in the form of metalliferous mud and polymetallic nodules. The importance of these deposits is promising for the not too distant future.

Oil wells

Minerals being exploited ★

Oil and natural gas exploitation ●

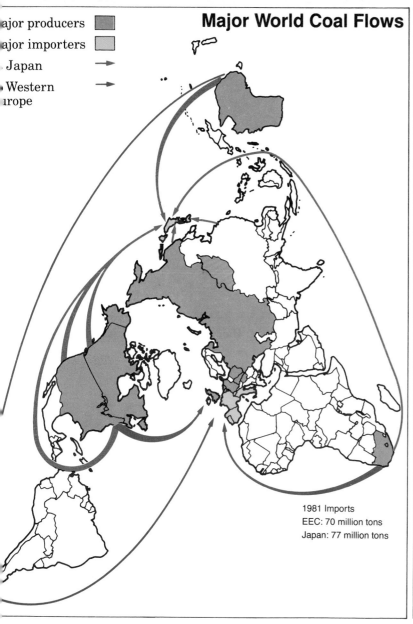

# Major World Coal Flows

1981 Imports
EEC: 70 million tons
Japan: 77 million tons

# Major World Oil Flows

OPEC countries

Major importers

From the Persian
Gulf

From the rest of the
world

Export zones

# Oil

Since the oil shocks of the 1970s, the demand for oil has slowed down considerably. Western consumption has been reduced by 25% in ten years. Production is now stagnant, at around 3 billion tons. The high-population Third World producers (Nigeria, Indonesia, Mexico, etc.) are suffering a severe recession after a few fat years. Saudi Arabia remains both the vital producer and the market regulator by virtue of its financial power.

| World Production | | Known Reserves (90 billion tons) | |
|---|---|---|---|
| 1955 | 7.72 million tons | Middle East | 54% |
| 1970 | 2.28 million tons | Saudi Arabia | 25% |
| 1978 | 3.09 million tons | Kuwait | 10% |
| 1981 | 3.05 million tons | Iran | 8% |
| | | Iraq | 5% |
| | | USSR | 11% |
| | | Mexico | 9% |
| | | USA | 4% |

## Producers

| | |
|---|---|
| USSR | 21% |
| Total Mid. East* | 32% |
| Saudi Arabia | 17% |
| Iraq | 1% |
| USA | 16% |
| Venezuela | 4% |
| Mexico | 4% |
| China | 3% |
| Nigeria | 2% |

*Includes Iran, Kuwait, Bahrain, United Arab Emirates, Oman.

# Coal

| Production | | Reserves | |
|---|---|---|---|
| USA | 25% | USA | 31% |
| USSR | 19% | USSR | 19% |
| China* | 24% | China | 25% |
| Poland | 5% | UK | 9% |
| UK | 4-5% | W. Germany | 4% |

*Combined coal and lignite.

# Lignite

| World Production | | Reserves | |
|---|---|---|---|
| GDR | 26% | USSR | 65% |
| USSR | 16% | USA | 7% |
| W. Germany | 13.5% | E. Germany | 10% |
| Czechoslovakia | 10% | W. Germany | 16% |

Since 1973, the rise in oil prices has given a boost to coal production, which had been growing slowly since 1955.

1955—1.6 billion tons
1973—2.3 billion tons
1980—3.3 billion tons

Reserves are enormous, probably 80% of all fossil energy reserves. The appearance of new techniques making possible the burning of coal in the deposits themselves seems likely to open up new possibilities.

Members of OPEC (Organization of Petroleum Exporting Countries). Thirteen countries. (Arab countries have formed OAPEC, Organization of Arab Petroleum Exporting Countries.) Initial members included: Iraq, Iran, Kuwait, Libya, Saudi Arabia, and Venezuela (1960). Others followed, including Qatar (1961), Indonesia (1962), Abu Dhabi and the United Arab Emirates (1967), Algeria (1969), Nigeria (1971), Ecuador (1973), Gabon (1975). The 13 states supply more than 50% of the world production of unrefined oil.

# Electricity*

## Hydroelectricity

| | |
|---|---|
| USA | 20% |
| Canada | 16% |
| USSR | 10% |
| Brazil<br>Japan<br>Norway<br>France<br>Sweden | } 4-5% each |

## Nuclear-powered Electricity**

| | 1980 | 1990 |
|---|---|---|
| USA | 37.5% | 28.5% |
| Japan | 11.7% | 7.7% |
| USSR | 10.0% | 17.5% |
| France | 8.7% | 12.8% |
| W. Germany | 6.2% | 5.4% |
| Canada | 5.7% | 3.2% |

*Electricity furnished by power stations using combustible fossil fuels is not included.

**Despite disputes and resistance, the progress in establishing power stations throughout the world is spectacular.

## Natural Gas

| Production | | Reserves | |
|---|---|---|---|
| USA | 35% | USSR | 40% |
| USSR | 30% | Iran | 18% |
| Netherlands | 5% | USA | 7% |
| Canada | 3% | Algeria | 4% |
| | | W. Europe | 5% |

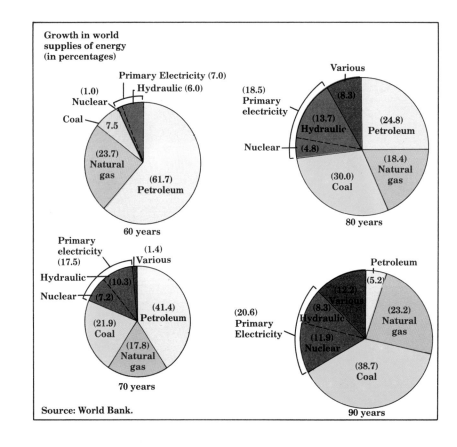

Growth in world supplies of energy (in percentages)

**60 years:** Primary Electricity (7.0), Hydraulic (6.0), Nuclear (1.0), Coal 7.5, Natural gas (23.7), Petroleum (61.7)

**80 years:** Various, (18.5) Primary electricity, Hydraulic (13.7), Nuclear (4.8), (8.3), Petroleum (24.8), Natural gas (18.4), Coal (30.0)

**70 years:** Primary electricity (17.5), Various (1.4), Hydraulic (10.3), Nuclear (7.2), Petroleum (41.4), Coal (21.9), Natural gas (17.8)

**90 years:** Petroleum (5.2), Various (12.2), (20.6) Primary Electricity, Hydraulic (8.3), Nuclear (11.9), Natural gas (23.2), Coal (38.7)

Source: World Bank.

# Energy Consumption per Capita
(In tons of petroleum)

| World Energy Production | | World Energy Consumption |
|---|---|---|
| 30% | Third World (including | 15% |
| 10% | oil exporting nations) | 0.6% |
| 38% | Developed nations (including Japan) | 54% |
| 32% | Eastern nations (including China) | 31% |

+ 6 tons

3 to 6 tons

1.5 to 3 tons

0.5 to 1.5 tons

less than 0.5 tons

North-South line

# Technological Levels

High-tech industries employ new and very advanced technologies that depend heavily on research and are produced by only a very small number of industrialized countries, which are anxious to retain the virtual monopoly of them and so guarantee their supremacy. Such industries include aeronautics and aerospace, telecommunications and telematics, nuclear energy, computers, and bio-industry.

## Data Processing (An example)

**Computers in Service in the USA (% of world total)**

| 1975 | 1980 | 2000 |
|---|---|---|
| 0.22 million | 1.25 million | 2.85 million |
| 65% | 65% | 40% |

**World Computer Market (1981)**

| | |
|---|---|
| USA | 73% |
| Japan | 10% |
| EEC | 16% |

**World Market for Electrical Components (1981)**

| | |
|---|---|
| USA | 48% |
| Japan | 27% |
| EEC | 23% |

High technology

Classic technology

Technological dependence

North-South lines

183

**Uranium**

# Uranium

The states that are big producers and possessors of large reserves* are few and concentrated in North America and the southern hemisphere. There are no reliable figures for China, the USSR, and Eastern Europe.

### Production

| | |
|---|---|
| USA | 33% |
| Canada | 17% |
| S. Africa | 13% |
| Namibia | 9% |
| Niger | 10% |
| France | 6% |
| Australia | 6% |

### Proved Reserves

Based on 5 million tons, except for the USSR, China, and Western countries that have reserves between 3.5 and 7 million tons.

| | |
|---|---|
| USA | 37% |
| Canada | 19% |
| S. Africa | 11% |
| Australia | 7% |
| Sweden | 6% |
| Niger | 5% |

### Percentage Share of World Industrial Power 1980
(as a percentage of the combined value of mining and manufacturing output)

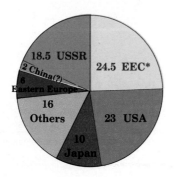

*EEC: FRG 9%, France 5.5%, United Kingdom 4.5%.

*Thorium, occasionally used as a substitute for uranium, is abundant in India (30%), Canada (20%), and Brazil (6%).

# World Grain Trade

**Major exporters**
**(% total exported)**

| | |
|---|---|
| USA | 54% |
| Canada | 12% |
| Argentina | 9% |
| France | 7% |
| Australia | 6% |

Producers-exporters

Importers

Principal flows

Chronic malnutrition     *

*Source:* World Bank.

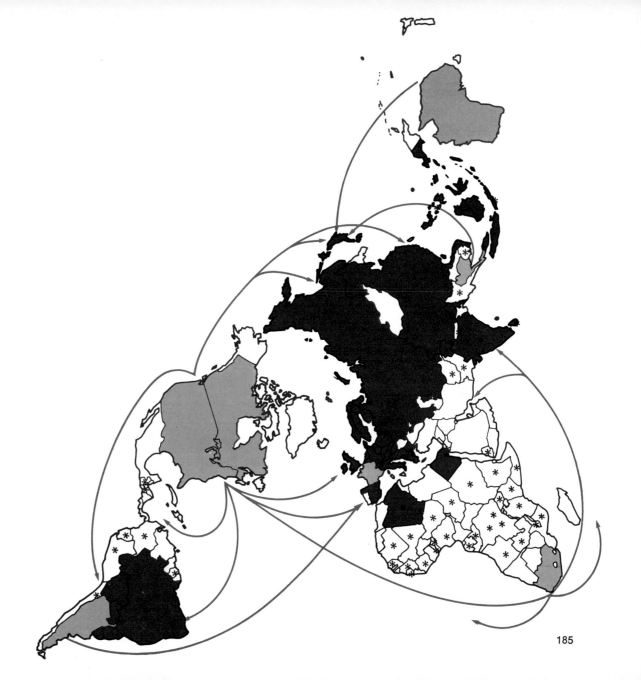

| World Cereal Producers* | | Major Cereals | |
|---|---|---|---|
| | | *Wheat* | |
| USA | 18% | USSR | 19.0% |
| China | 17% | USA | 14.5% |
| USSR | 10% | China | 12.0% |
| India | 9% | | |
| France | 3% | *Corn* | |
| Canada | 3% | USA | 46% |
| | | China | 13% |
| | | Brazil | 5% |
| **Soya** | | *Rice* | |
| USA | 63% | China | 35% |
| Brazil | 17% | India | 20% |
| China | 9% | Indonesia | 8% |

*Calculated on the basis of 8 cereals: wheat, rice, corn, barley, rye, oats, buckwheat, millet.

# Fertilizers

Chemical fertilizers are now intensively used in countries with a modern agriculture to ensure high and regular yields, and also to combat soil deterioration.

The major fertilizer producers are the USA, the USSR, the EEC (more than half the total), and Canada.

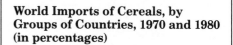

**World Imports of Cereals, by Groups of Countries, 1970 and 1980 (in percentages)**

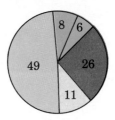

1970 = 109 million tons

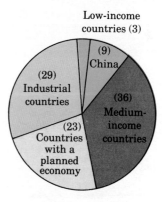

1980 = 228 million tons

*Source:* World Bank.

## Livestock

The real value of livestock is difficult to compare because of the enormous variety of species and modes of stock-rearing. High-productivity Danish cattle-rearing and the livestock of India, for example, have nothing in common.

Over the last two decades, factory farming of chickens and pigs has vastly increased in the developed countries, largely replacing traditional methods of husbandry.

| Cattle | | Sheep | | Pigs | |
|---|---|---|---|---|---|
| India | 15% | USSR | 13% | China | 38% |
| USSR | 10% | Australia | 12% | USSR | 10% |
| USA | 9% | China | 9% | USA | 8.5% |
| Brazil | 7.5% | N. Zealand | 6% | Brazil | 5% |
| China | 5% | | | | |
| Argentina | 5% | | | | |

Pigs •

Sheep •

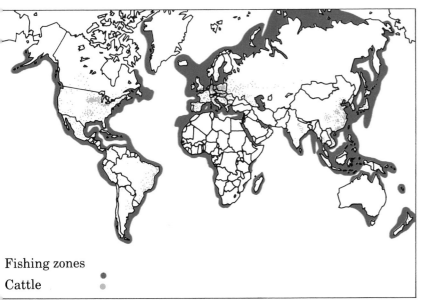

Fishing zones •

Cattle •

## Fishing

Fishing supplies about 10% of humanity's protein requirements. In addition to food, industrial fishing produces a number of products used in industry: flours, oils, grease, etc.

If maritime states extend the limits of their territorial waters to 200 nautical miles, the industrial and deep-sea fishing activities of other states are likely to be severely handicapped.

| | |
|---|---|
| Japan | 14.6% |
| USSR | 12.5% |
| China | 5.8% |
| USA | 5% |
| Chile | 4% |
| Peru | 4% |
| Norway | 4% |

# POPULATION FACTORS

# Population by Major Regions in the Second Half of the 20th Century: 1950–1975–Projection 2000

*Source: Global 2000 Report to the President,* Washington, DC; and the World Bank.

## World Population 1800-2000

| Year | In millions |
|------|-------------|
| 1800 | 900 |
| 1850 | 1100 |
| 1900 | 1600 |
| 1950 | 2600 |
| 1980 | 4400 |
| 2000 | 6100 |

Australia, N. Zealand
& the Pacific
1950 : 11
1975 : 18
2000 : 23

Japan
1950 : 83
1975 : 117
2000 : 130

Southeast
Asia
1950 : 215
1975 : 395
2000 : 590

USSR &
East Europe
1950 : 275
1975 : 410
2000 : 470

China
1950 : 560
1975 : 975
2000 : 1250

Indian
Subcontinent
1950 : 480
1975 : 933
2000 : 1380

North
America
1950 : 170
1975 : 251
2000 : 285

Middle East
1950 : 55
1975 : 135
2000 : 220

Latin
America
1950 : 152
1975 : 353
2000 : 530

Western
Europe
1950 : 315
1975 : 346
2000 : 375

Africa
1950 : 222
1975 : 467
2000 : 830

189

## Most Populous States: Evolution of Their Population, 1930 to 2000 (est.)

|              | 1930 | 1950 | 1980 | 2000 |
|--------------|-----:|-----:|-----:|-----:|
| China        | 430  | 540  | 970  | 1240 |
| India        | 335  | 370  | 673  | 975  |
| USSR         | 160  | 180  | 265  | 315  |
| USA          | 120  | 155  | 227  | 260  |
| Indonesia    | 60   | 77   | 146  | 220  |
| Brazil       | 40   | 53   | 119  | 177  |
| Bangladesh   |      | 40   | 92   | 148  |
| Pakistan     |      | 35   | 82   | 141  |
| Nigeria      | 19   | 28   | 85   | 161  |
| Japan        | 64   | 84   | 117  | 130  |
| Mexico       | 16   | 26   | 67   | 110  |
| Vietnam      | 22   | 25   | 54   | 88   |
| Philippines  | 12   | 20   | 48   | 75   |
| Thailand     | 11   | 19   | 46   | 68   |
| Turkey       | 11   | 21   | 45   | 70   |
| Iran         | 14   | 20   | 38   | 64   |
| Egypt        | 14   | 21   | 40   | 61   |
| Italy        | 41   | 47   | 57   | 61   |

Evolution of rhythm of world increase (mean annual rate)

1800-1850: 0.55%
1850-1900: 0.57%
1900-1950: 0.83%
1950-1980: 1.87%
1980-2000: 1.80% est.

## AGE AND SEX OF THE WORLD POPULATION, 1975 AND 2000

Developed countries

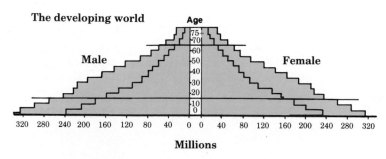

The developing world

*Source: Global 2000 Report to the President,* Washington, DC, 1980.

# World Urbanization

+ 75%

+ 50%

+ 35%

− 35%

Empty regions

Depopulated areas are shown
for the USSR, Canada,
Australia.

# Urbanization

## The Major Cities or Concentrations of the World

| 1900 | | 1950 | | 2000 (est.) | |
|---|---|---|---|---|---|
| London | 6.4 | New York | 12.3 | Mexico | 31 |
| New York | 4.2 | London | 10.4 | S. Paulo | 25.8 |
| Paris | 3.9 | Rhine-Ruhr | 6.9 | Shanghai | 23.7 |
| Berlin | 2.4 | Tokyo | 6.7 | Tokyo-Yokohama | 23.1 |
| Chicago | 1.7 | Shanghai | 5.8 | New York | 22.4 |
| Vienna | 1.6 | Paris | 5.5 | Peking | 20.9 |
| Tokyo | 1.4 | Buenos Aires | 5.3 | Rio | 19 |
| St Petersburg | 1.4 | Chicago | 4.9 | Bombay | 16.8 |
| Philadelphia | 1.4 | Moscow | 4.8 | Calcutta | 16.4 |
| Manchester | 1.2 | Calcutta | 4.6 | Jakarta | 15.7 |
| Birmingham | 1.2 | Los Angeles | 4 | Los Angeles | 13.9 |
| Moscow | 1.2 | Osaka | 3.8 | Seoul | 13.7 |
| Peking | 1.1 | Milan | 3.6 | Cairo | 12.9 |
| Calcutta | 1 | Bombay | 3 | Madras | 12.7 |
| Boston | 1 | Mexico | 3 | Buenos Aires | 12.1 |
| Glasgow | 1 | Philadelphia | 4 | Karachi | 11.6 |
| Liverpool | 0.98 | Rio | 2.9 | Delhi | 11.5 |
| Osaka | 0.95 | Detroit | 2.8 | Manila | 11.4 |
| Constantinople | 0.92 | Naples | 2.6 | Teheran | 11.1 |
| Hamburg | 0.9 | Leningrad | 2.5 | Baghdad | 11 |

*(In millions of inhabitants; the powerful industrial cities are underlined.)*

## URBAN POPULATION

*Source:* World Bank.

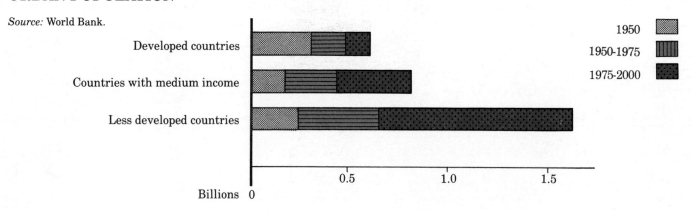

Legend:
- 1950
- 1950-1975
- 1975-2000

Developed countries

Countries with medium income

Less developed countries

Billions  0    0.5    1.0    1.5

# NORTH–SOUTH

As capitalism introduced modernizing elements abroad, it dislocated the traditional economies of the dominated countries. These distortions lie at the origin of what is called underdevelopment. In fact, the Third World covers very diverse realities, although it is possible to list a number of common traits: preponderance of the agricultural sector, high birth rate, very marked economic and social inequalities. Over the last two decades, the Third World has seen growing differentiations caused by both the level of local productive forces and/or the significance of mineral resources, particularly oil and natural gas. Outside a handful of countries that have seen high growth rates, the majority of Third World countries have made little progress and have generally stagnated or even regressed. In a majority of countries, agriculture, which still employs the bulk of the population, cannot satisfy local needs. Deterioration in the terms of trade that has marked the three decades following World War II continues to weigh heavily. Only the OPEC countries, producers of oil and natural gas, were able to modify the laws of the market during the decade 1973 to 1983.

Population growth, which has since the beginning of the century been consistently high in the Third World, continues at a rate approaching 3%. World population, estimated at 4 billion ten years ago, will pass 6 billion by the end of the century. At that date, peoples of the Third World will make up 80% of the globe's population, whereas they were only 65% in 1970. The living conditions of the 2.5 billion people who live in the Third World have scarcely improved in twenty years, while 880 million of them are considered to be living in conditions well below subsistence. The reforms proposed by international organizations concerned with development run up against both the unequal North–South system and the political impediments constituted by the ruling strata in the Third World. Up to now, the countries that have recorded notable growth are the oil-producing countries, especially those with small populations, like Kuwait, Saudi Arabia, the United Arab Emirates, and Libya; a handful of countries, such as Brazil or Gabon (underpopulated) that have large mineral resources; and a series of Asian countries where the quality of manpower and business abilities are of a high order: Taiwan, Singapore, South Korea, Thailand, etc.

Today, there are three categories of countries in the Third World: those few that have a high or relatively high growth rate, some of which already have a significant industrial infrastructure; a sizable proportion of average countries that are developing despite a high population growth; and about fifty classified as less developed countries (LDCs) whose situation is tragic. The current crisis is hitting the Third World very hard. Africa seems particularly threatened in every respect: stagnation, or even regression of growth, galloping population growth, corruption, and the ineffectiveness of the vast majority of ruling strata. In Andean America (Ecuador, Peru, Bolivia, etc.), the situation—and the prospects—are scarcely any better. In Southeast Asia, alongside not insignificant growth and dynamic industrial sectors, there remain, especially in the Indian subcontinent (Bangladesh, India, Pakistan), enormous areas of poverty and malnutrition.

**Evolution of GNP by Main World Regions 1975—Projection 2000**
(In dollars per capita)

Australia
N. Zealand
1975 : 4900
2000 : 10000

Japan
1975 : 4100
2000 : 10000

China
1975 : 200
2000 : 540

USSR &
East. Europe
1975 : 2590
2000 : 4800

Southeast
Asia
1975 : 340
2000 : 600

North
America
1975 : 7100
2000 : 14500

Indian
Subcontinent
1975 : 135
2000 : 300

Middle East
1975 : 1600
2000 : 4000 (?)

Latin
America
1975 : 950
2000 : 1700

Western
Europe
1975 : 4500
2000 : 10000

Africa
1975 : 310
2000 : 600

Source: *Global 2000 Report to the President*, Washington, DC, 1980

# Income
# Health
# Education
# 1950-1980

## Income

| GNP per person (1980 dollars) | 1950 | 1960 | 1980 |
|---|---|---|---|
| Industrial countries | 4,130 | 5,580 | 10,660 |
| Medium-income countries | 640 | 820 | 1,580 |
| Low-income countries | 170 | 180 | 250 |

| Mean annual increase (%) | 1950-1960 | 1960-1980 |
|---|---|---|
| Industrial countries | 3.1 | 3.3 |
| Medium-income countries | 2.5 | 3.3 |
| Low-income countries | 0.6 | 1.7 |

## Health

*Life expectancy at birth (years)*

| | 1950 | 1960 | 1979 | Increase 1950-79 |
|---|---|---|---|---|
| Industrial countries | 67 | 70 | 74 | 7 |
| Medium-income countries | 48 | 53 | 61 | 13 |
| Low-income countries | 37 | 42 | 51 | 14 |
| Planned economies | 60 | 68 | 72 | 12 |

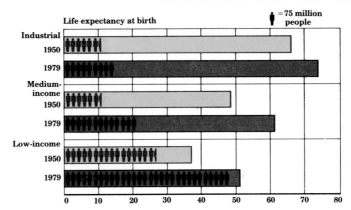

## Education

*Adult literacy rate (%)*

| | 1950 | 1960 | 1976 |
|---|---|---|---|
| Industrial countries | 95 | 97 | 99 |
| Medium-income countries | 48 | 53 | 72 |
| Low-income countries | 22 | 28 | 39 |
| Planned economies | 97 | 97 | 99 |

*Note:* China is not included.

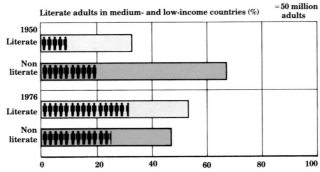

*Source:* World Bank.

# Evolution of Food Consumption (1970–1980)

According to the World Bank, 800 million people in the Third World live below the threshold of absolute poverty and suffer from undernourishment or grave malnutrition, especially in Asia and subtropical Africa.

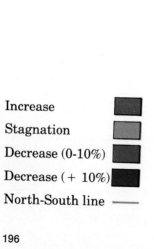

Increase

Stagnation

Decrease (0-10%)

Decrease (+ 10%)

North-South line

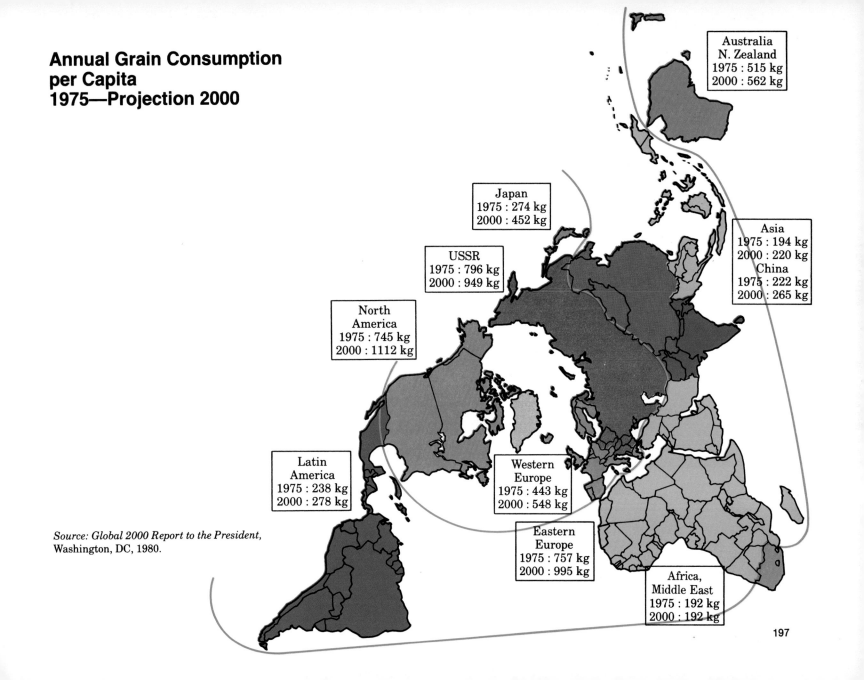

**Annual Grain Consumption
per Capita
1975—Projection 2000**

Australia
N. Zealand
1975 : 515 kg
2000 : 562 kg

Japan
1975 : 274 kg
2000 : 452 kg

Asia
1975 : 194 kg
2000 : 220 kg
China
1975 : 222 kg
2000 : 265 kg

USSR
1975 : 796 kg
2000 : 949 kg

North
America
1975 : 745 kg
2000 : 1112 kg

Latin
America
1975 : 238 kg
2000 : 278 kg

Western
Europe
1975 : 443 kg
2000 : 548 kg

Eastern
Europe
1975 : 757 kg
2000 : 995 kg

Africa,
Middle East
1975 : 192 kg
2000 : 192 kg

*Source: Global 2000 Report to the President,*
Washington, DC, 1980.

197

# Major World Industrial Regions

Industrial regions ▢

North-South line ——

# The Third World: East–West Struggle

What is the interim balance sheet of East–West competition in the Third World?

The period immediately after World War II was favorable to the Communist forces in Asia: in China totally, in Korea partly. After a long rearguard action waged by the French and the Americans, the upholders of "Marxism–Leninism" won a major success in Indochina, of which Vietnam was the major beneficiary.

Conversely, in Indonesia in 1965, the largest Communist party in Asia was decimated. Over time, the economic situation of the regional allies (Taiwan, Singapore, South Korea, Thailand, Malaysia) of the United States improved.

The recognition of China in 1971 (after a decade of Sino-Soviet conflict), as a result of the Nixon-Kissinger initiative, enabled the United States to engage in a three-sided game advantageous to it.

In the Middle East, compared with the Baghdad Pact (Turkey, Iraq, Iran, Pakistan) period, the West has suffered serious setbacks. The fall of the Shah in Iran was a major setback for the USA. But after the long alliance during the Nasser period, the breach precipitated by Egypt (1972) was just as serious for the USSR, whose Arab policy has run into difficulties (Iraq) and is only very partially effective (Syria, PLO) in a situation where, up till now, the United States continues to be in the position of arbiter. Israel, a close ally of the United States, remains the major military power in the region, while Saudi Arabia, whose stability is vital for the West, has played a moderating role among the oil-producing countries.

Russian occupation of Afghanistan, conversely, weakened the United States ally Pakistan, whereas India has succeeded since Nehru in making the best use of the delicate notion of nonalignment.

The Western preserve that Africa had been up to 1975, despite various Soviet attempts (from Guinea 1959, to Sudan and Somalia in the early 1970s) is now an integral part of the East-West confrontation. In Angola (1975) and Ethiopia (1977), the presence of Cuban troops added an altogether new dimension to the Soviet presence. Mozambique can be included among the allies of the USSR. Other African countries, sometimes classified as allies of the USSR, seem to be in a much more ambiguous situation: Congo, Guinea-Bissau, Madagascar, etc. On the continent as a whole, the West continues to be predominant.

In Latin America, the United States (except during the Carter administration) has essentially maintained its role as policeman: Directly or indirectly, the policy of the "big stick" has been used in Guatemala (1954), without success in Cuba (1961), in the Dominican Republic (1965), in the training of counterinsurgency forces throughout the continent to deal with the guerrilla movements of the 1960s, as well as in Brazil (1964) and Chile (1973).

The new factor, since the 1979 victory of the Sandinistas in Nicaragua (made easier by American neutrality), is the increase in the number of large-scale armed struggles in Central America (El Salvador, Guatemala). These guerrilla wars, born of local economic situations, enable the USSR and Cuba to challenge Washington in its own backyard, the Caribbean basin, which is vital for the geostrategic security of the United States.

Overall, it is less a U.S. retreat (in any case only relative and altogether normal, given the fact that the United States held a virtually worldwide hegemony in a situation of complete military superiority) than the transformation of the USSR from a regional power into a truly world power, that is the major change of the last three decades.

In this new context, it goes without saying that the world crisis, felt particularly in the Third World and aggravated by the fecklessness of the ruling strata in many countries, will make the confrontations sharper.

THE MOVEMENT OF THE NONALIGNED
Created in 1961 at the Belgrade Conference.

*Latin America:* Argentina, Bolivia, Peru, Ecuador, Panama, Nicaragua, Cuba, Jamaica, Guyana (ex-British), Surinam, Trinidad and Tobago, Grenada, Barbados and St. Lucia.

*Africa:* All states except Namibia, South Africa, and Western Sahara (ex-Spanish); the Cape Verde Islands, São Tomé and Principe, Mauritius, the Comoros, and the Seychelles.

*Europe:* Yugoslavia, Malta, and Cyprus.

*Middle East:* All the Arab states, Iran, Afghanistan.

*Indian subcontinent:* Pakistan, India, Nepal, Bhutan, Bangladesh, Sri Lanka, the Maldives.

*East Asia:* Laos, Vietnam, Cambodia, Malaysia, Indonesia, Singapore, North Korea.

*Le Groupe des 77:* An organization for economic order concerned with North-South relations; includes 120 members (1980) including all the countries of the Third World except China, Namibia, Western Sahara (ex-Spanish), and Turkey. Also members: Yugoslavia, Romania.

# Arms Sales to Third World Countries

The leading arms exporters are: the United States (37%), the USSR (30%), France (8%), and Great Britain and West Germany (5% each).

The major arms importers are in the Middle East (40%). If members of NATO (12%) and the Warsaw Pact (12%) are excluded, the other importers are Africa (17%), Asia (11%), Latin America (5%). In order of quantity, the main purchasers are Saudi Arabia, Jordan, Iraq, Syria, Libya, South Korea, India, Israel, Vietnam, Morocco, and Ethiopia. These countries (plus Iran*) buy almost a third of the total arms sold in Asia, Africa, and Latin America.

---

*It is difficult to know what place Iran occupies at present.

# Indebtedness: A Factor Aggravating the Crisis

**Total Public Debt, Third World Countries, 1982: $575 billion* (1973: $98 billion)**

*Most indebted states:*
(Public debt and pledges in $ billions)

| | | | |
|---|---|---|---|
| Brazil | 43.8 | Algeria | 14.4 |
| Mexico | 42.7 | Egypt | 13.8 |
| Poland | 27(?) | Turkey | 13.8 |
| S. Korea | 20.0 | Israel | 13.8 |
| India | 18.5 | Venezuela | 11.3 |
| Indonesia | 15.5 | Argentina | 10.0 |

**Eastern European Countries Public Debt: $80 billion (1973: $8 billion)**

*Interest payments—$31 billion in 1980—doubled between 1978 and 1980.

The changes that have occurred in the debt structure of developing countries contrast with the stability of its distribution. Since 1973, it is the same twelve major borrowers who owe almost two-thirds of the debt and debt servicing, each of them having at present a debt of over 12 billion dollars. Five of these debtors—Algeria, Egypt, Indonesia, Mexico and Venezuela—are oil-exporting countries. The other seven—Argentina, Brazil, India, Israel, Korea, Turkey, and Yugoslavia—are major exporters of manufactures.

It is middle-income countries that accounted for most of the debt of developing countries (349 billion dollars out of a total of 410 billion dollars) at the end of 1980. About 70% of their debt had been incurred from private sources.

Conversely, at the end of 1980, 87% of the debt of low-income countries had been contracted from public sources; out of net transfers of 5 billion dollars made to these countries during 1980, public sources of financing supplied 88%. Whereas the total amount of flows to these countries increased by 55% in 1980 to reach 13.5 billion dollars, those made by multilateral institutions almost doubled (and reached 6.4 billion dollars).

*Source:* World Bank.

## External Public Debt
(In % of GNP for states of each group)

**Poor countries:** 19.2% (1970: 15.6%)

**Middle-income countries:**
Petroleum importers: 15.4% (1970: 10.7%)
Petroleum exporters: 21.3% (1970: 14%)

**Eastern countries:** no data

**Yugoslavia:** 6.6% (1970: 8.8%)

80% of the debt of the private banking system to countries in the process of development is held by 20 developed countries, and 50% by only five among those: the United States, Canada, the United Kingdom, France, and West Germany.

## Remittances of Funds Received by Labor-Exporting Countries

| Major Countries | Amount in $ Billions | Remittance of Funds as % of Exports of Merchandise |
|---|---|---|
| Yugoslavia | 4.8 | 70 |
| Turkey | 2.0 | 71 |
| Italy | 3.2 | 2 |
| Algeria | 0.5 | 3 |
| Spain | 1.2 | 6 |
| Tunisia | 0.3 | 17 |
| India | 1.2 | 18 |
| Pakistan | 2.0 | 80 |
| Greece | 1.0 | 26 |
| Morocco | 1.0 | 44 |
| Portugal | 2.9 | 64 |
| Jordan | 0.8 | 138 |
| Egypt | 2.6 | 220 |
| S. Yemen | 0.3 | 715 |
| Yemen | 1.3 | 995 |

*Source:* OECD, 1980.

# THE MILITARY BALANCE

# The Military Balance

Compiling a balance sheet using tables listing the armed might of the protagonists is only one approach.*

This statistical listing, though very useful, is only one admittedly vital factor in a balance in which sociopolitical factors, attitudes, and will remain of fundamental importance. Traditionally, the listings are measured by experts, but strategies are won with peoples and leaders.

For thirty-five years, generalized war has been avoided through the balance of terror. Conflicts have taken place in the framework of indirect strategies, in local conventional wars, or still more often in guerrilla movements or crisis management without overt conflict (Berlin, Cuba).

During the last twenty years, since the Cuban missile crisis (1962), the USSR has greatly increased its military might in the air, on the sea, and in the nuclear domain.

In the present state of affairs, while nuclear war seems highly improbable, nations must act as if it were possible (at least by accident)—hence the need, in the arms race, to be constantly improving their panoply of weapons.

If, in short, it is agreed that nuclear war, launched in cold blood, is not at present (but for how long?) conceivable, each side has to respond to the expectations of the other. In this respect, today as yesterday, strategy rests on a "dialectic of uncertainties" (Lucien Poirier).

But strategy is not limited to war—far from it. It aims above all at producing psychological effects on peoples.

In connection with a possible resumption of discussions on arms control and reduction (SALT I, 1972), everything points to the conclusion that the installation of SS-20s by the Soviets (1977) was a coercive strategy, intended, through the prospect of the threat of a nuclear war, to lead to the neutralization of Western Europe vis-à-vis the United States—what in the jargon is called political uncoupling.

The SS-20† is not a weapon of deterrence but of pressure on Western Europe and especially on West Germany, its Achilles' heel. In this sense, the debate on the installation of Pershing 2s is first of all a problem of political will for Europeans.

---

*In addition, figures are quickly out of date. See *The Military Balance* by the International Institute of Strategic Studies, London, which annually provides figures on the world military balance, nation by nation.

---

†Each SS-20 carries three independently targeted nuclear warheads, with very great firepower. Carrying 150 kilotons in each nuclear warhead, the SS-20 has a range of 2,700 nautical miles. At present, the USSR has 300 SS-20s. Experts estimate that 150 SS-20s could destroy the whole of NATO's defense system in Europe.

# Strategic Nuclear Arsenals

|  | USA | USSR |
|---|---|---|
| Intercontinental missiles | 1,052 | 1,398 |
| Nuclear warheads | 2,152 | 5,230 |
| Strategic ballistic missiles, submarine launched | 520 On board 36 nuclear-powered submarines | 969 On board 80 nuclear-powered submarines |
| Nuclear warheads | 4,768 | 1,752 |
| Continental strategic missiles, surface to surface | * | 740 Of which 80% are west of the Urals |
| Strategic bombers | 376 Of which 316 are long-range | 150 Of which 105 are long-range |

*Source: Military Balance, 1982–83.*

---

*Pershing 2s and ground-launched cruise missiles are, in principle, to be installed in West Germany, Great Britain, Italy, Belgium, and the Netherlands.

France has 80 submarine-launched strategic missiles (range 3,000 km, with one nuclear warhead per missile, aboard 5 nuclear-powered submarines). It also has 18 intermediate-range strategic missiles (3,500 km) and 36 strategic bombers.

Great Britain has 64 submarine-launched strategic missiles (range 4,000 km, with three thermonuclear warheads per missile, aboard 4 nuclear-powered submarines).

As far as tactical nuclear forces are concerned, the Atlantic Alliance has 348 surface-to-surface missiles against 1,980 for the Warsaw Pact countries, and 603 airplanes against 2,650.

|  | Atlantic Alliance | Warsaw Pact |
|---|---|---|
| Nuclear attack submarines | 90 | 99 |
| Combat vessels, tonnage | 3.385* | 2.685* |
| Aircraft carriers | 18 | 4 |
| Vessels of over 2,000 tons | 348 | 139 |
| Amphibious vessels, tonnage | 759* | 141* |
| Navy planes | 2,600 | 750 |

*In millions of tons.

The comparisons reflect only very imperfectly the actual forces, even numerically, as far as air and land potentials are concerned. The American and Soviet tank and airborne divisions have quite different compositions. In fact, no one doubts the superiority of the Warsaw Pact's conventional forces in the European theater.

From the point of view of naval potential, the superiority of the Atlantic Alliance is beyond doubt, control of the seas being vital to the West.

# Deployment of United States Naval Forces

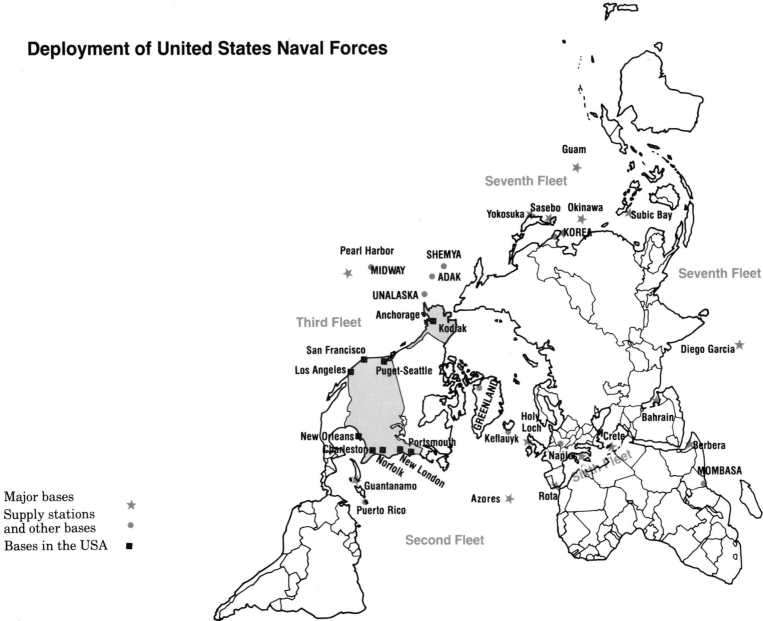

Guam

**Seventh Fleet**

Yokosuka   Sasebo   Okinawa   Subic Bay

KOREA

Pearl Harbor   SHEMYA

MIDWAY   ADAK

UNALASKA

Anchorage

Kodiak

**Third Fleet**

San Francisco

Los Angeles   Puget-Seattle

New Orleans

Charleston   Portsmouth

Norfolk   New London

Guantanamo

Puerto Rico

GREENLAND

Keflauyk

Holy Loch

Naples

Crete

Bahrain

Berbera

MOMBASA

Azores

Rota

**Sixth Fleet**

**Seventh Fleet**

Diego Garcia

**Second Fleet**

Major bases           ★
Supply stations
and other bases       ●
Bases in the USA      ■

205

# Soviet World Naval Deployment and Supply Stations

This deployment is in effect despite seasonally frozen seas:
- toward the Atlantic from the White Sea and the Kola Peninsula
- toward the Pacific from the Siberian coast (Vladivostok–Petropavlovsk)

The military ports in the Baltic and the Black Sea (semi-closed seas) have seen their role decline.

The Soviet naval presence is particularly large in the Indian Ocean.

Vietnam and Cuba provide particularly reliable supply stations.

| | |
|---|---|
| Major supply stations | ■ |
| Other supply stations | □ |
| Soviet military ports | ● |
| Allies of the USSR | |

# The Sea and Sea Power

The sea is the most widely used means of communications and trade, and the volume of trade has continuously increased over recent decades. The West—and Japan—depend heavily on freedom of navigation.

As a result of recent technological progress, the sea, a traditional source of wealth from fishing, has become an object of conflict, and disputes over the limits of sovereignty have increased. Offshore petroleum already accounts for a third of world production. But the very near prospect of the exploitation of significant ocean mineral resources is awakening appetities.

The Maritime Convention adopted in 1982 by most countries—but not by the United States, which is the best equipped technologically to exploit undersea riches—stipulates that territorial waters extend 12 miles and that states exercise sovereign rights (especially economic ones) up to a 200-mile limit.

During the 1970s, the rise of Soviet sea power, the result of two decades of effort, was one of the main factors changing the East-West balance, which had previously been almost exclusively limited to the land theater. From 1961 onward, the Soviet fleet progressively extended its presence, and by 1975 it was a worldwide force.

American naval superiority remains undeniable, but "the U.S. Navy must keep open the lines of communication without which the United States could not live, while the Soviet fleet does not have to protect vital lines of communication but only to cut those of its adversary" (Courtau-Bégarie). The new world order is largely being played out on the seas, with their resources and their bases.

## WORLDWIDE DEPLOYMENT OF AMERICAN NAVAL FORCES

*Second Fleet (Atlantic)*
Major bases: *Norfolk*, Charleston, Jacksonville, New Orleans, Puerto Rico, Boston, New London, Brunswick (Portland)
- 72 submarines (with 31 missile launchers)
- 76 major combat vessels
Units of this fleet are at Guantanamo (Cuba), Bermuda, Keflavik (Iceland), Holy Loch (GB).

*Third Fleet (Eastern Pacific)*
Major bases: *Pearl Harbor* (Hawaii), San Francisco, San Diego, Whidbey I., Long Beach (Los Angeles), Adak (Alaska)
- 35 submarines (with 5 missile launchers)
- 47 major combat vessels

*Sixth Fleet (Mediterranean)*
Principal bases: Gaeta, Naples (Italy), Rota (Spain)
- 5 submarines
- 16 major combat vessels

*Seventh Fleet (Western Pacific)*\*
Major bases: Yokosuka (Japan), Subic Bay (Philippines), Guam, Midway
- 8 submarines
- 23 major combat vessels

\*A certain number of combat vessels are in the Indian Ocean and the Persian Gulf area (about 20 surface vessels)

*Note:* Below the names of the fleets appear their bases or base areas. The headquarters of the fleets are shown in italics.

# WORLDWIDE DEPLOYMENT OF SOVIET NAVAL FORCES

*North Fleet*
*Severomorsk,* Kola, White Sea
• 135 submarines (with 45 missile launchers)
•  82 major combat vessels

*Baltic Fleet*
*Baltiysk,* Kronstadt, Riga, Tallin
• 22 submarines
• 42 major combat vessels

*Black Sea Fleet*
*Sebastopol,* Odessa, Poti
• 22 submarines
• 84 major combat vessels
(The Soviet squadron operating in the Mediterranean is included in this fleet.)

*Pacific Fleet*
Vladivostok, Petropavlosk, Sov. Gavan
• 80 submarines (with 24 missile launchers)
• 86 major combat vessels
(Elements of this fleet are stationed or operating in Vietnam—Camh Ranh, Danang—and in the Indian Ocean—Socotra, Aden, Kahlak, etc.)

*Note:* Below the names of the fleets appear their bases or base areas. The headquarters of the fleets are shown in italics.

# AMERICAN MILITARY ABROAD*

| **Total** | **469,711** |
| *Land* | *446,043* |
| *Sea* | *23,668* |

| Europe | 328,577 | Western Hemisphere | 16,642 |
|---|---|---|---|
| Far East & Pacific | 124,492 | At sea | 2,138 |
| At sea | 21,530 | Panama | 9,616 |
| Japan | 47,269 | Guantanamo | 2,163 |
| S. Korea | 39,317 | Other | 2,725 |
| Philippines | 15,414 | | |
| Australia | 636 | | |
| Other | 326 | | |

# SOVIET MILITARY PRESENCE AND ALLIES, WORLDWIDE (1982)*

**Strong presence Soviet bloc technicians or military advisers**

| Ethiopia | 3,000-3,500 | Cuba |
|---|---|---|
| Afghanistan | 7,000-8,000 | USSR |
| Algeria | 2,000-3,000 | USSR |
| Libya | 2,000 | USSR |
| Syria | 2,000 | USSR |
| South Yemen | 1,500 | USSR |
| Nicaragua | 1,000 | Cuba |

# SOVIET BLOC TROOPS ABROAD

| | Country | Number | Since |
|---|---|---|---|
| USSR | Afghanistan | 100,000 | 1979 |
| Cuba | Angola | 15,000-20,000 | 1975 |
| | Ethiopia | 7,000-9,000 | 1977 |
| Vietnam | Cambodia | 180,000 | 1978 |

*Source:* U.S. Department of State.

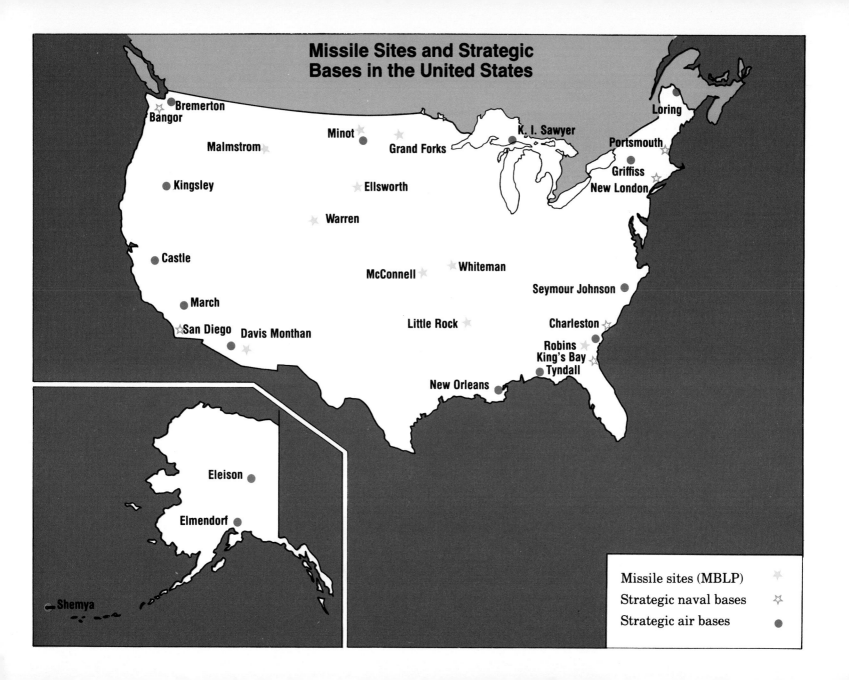

# Missile Sites and Strategic Bases in the United States

Bremerton
Bangor
Minot
Malmstrom
Grand Forks
K. I. Sawyer
Loring
Portsmouth
Griffiss
New London
Kingsley
Ellsworth
Warren
Castle
McConnell
Whiteman
Seymour Johnson
March
Little Rock
Charleston
San Diego
Davis Monthan
Robins
King's Bay
Tyndall
New Orleans

Eleison
Elmendorf
Shemya

Missile sites (MBLP)
Strategic naval bases
Strategic air bases

# Location of Soviet Ballistic Missile Sites

*Map supplied by General P. Gallois.*

# The USA under the Threat of Soviet Missiles

Positions occupied by
Soviet submarine
missile launchers able
to hit the territory of
the USA in 1970. No
major change in 1980.

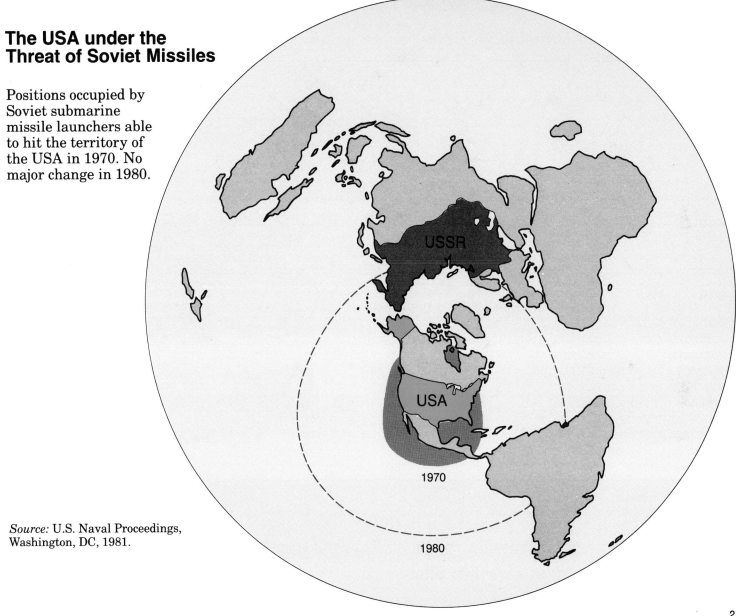

*Source:* U.S. Naval Proceedings,
Washington, DC, 1981.

## The USSR under the Threat of American Missiles

Distance at which American missiles had to be in 1970 to hit Soviet territory.
Their position in 1980 to hit the same target (Trident I). Before 1990, Trident II will make it possible to extend the firing range farther.

*Source:* U.S. Naval Proceedings, Washington, DC, 1981.

## Space

Surveillance is currently the most important military application of space. Satellites make it possible to watch enemy missile bases and thus to shorten the warning time. Satellites equipped with cameras move on an orbit that varies between 150 and 500 km high.

### Conquest of Space
*Largely dominated by the U.S. and the USSR*

| Year | 1951–1960 | 1961–1965 | 1966–1970 | 1971–1975 | 1976–1980 | 1981 | Total |
|------|------|------|------|------|------|------|-------|
| USA  | 31   | 239  | 244  | 135  | 111  | 18   | 778   |
| USSR | 9    | 121  | 335  | 413  | 461  | 98   | 1,437 |

Table of successful space launches (1957-1981). 1982 (Jan.–April): U.S., 8; USSR, 29.

## PRINCIPAL BENEFICIARIES OF AMERICAN MILITARY AID (1950-1980)
### (In billions of dollars)

### ESF

| World total: | 28 |
|---|---|
| Israel | 4 |
| Egypt | 4 |
| S. Korea | 2 |
| Turkey | 1 |
| Jordan | 0.9 |

### FMS

| World total: | 22 |
|---|---|
| Israel | 12 |
| Egypt | 1.5 |
| S. Korea | 1.2 |
| Turkey | 1 |
| Greece | 1 |
| Taiwan | 0.5 |
| Iran | 0.5 |
| Spain | 0.5 |
| Jordan | 0.4 |

### IMET

| World total: | 2 |
|---|---|
| S. Vietnam | 0.3 |
| S. Korea | 0.2 |
| Turkey | 0.1 |
| Thailand | 0.1 |

### MAP

| World total: | 54 |
|---|---|
| S. Vietnam | 14.8 |
| S. Korea | 5.3 |
| France | 4 |
| Turkey | 3.1 |
| Taiwan | 2.6 |
| Italy | 2 |

**ESF**   Economic support fund
**FMS**   Foreign military sales financing program
**IMET**   International military education and training program
**MAP**   Military assistance program

## FORCES FACE-TO-FACE IN THE EUROPEAN THEATER (1982)

NATO
(excluding Canada, including France)
*American forces stationed in Europe*
• Total strength: 0.22 million (0.20 million in FRG)
• Tanks: about 1,000
• Planes: more than 800
• Sixth Fleet (Mediterranean)
• Units of the Second Fleet (Holy Loch, GB)

*European forces (NATO)*
• Total strength: 2.2 million
• Tanks: about 16,000
• Fighter planes: about 3,700
• 260 major surface vessels, 143 submarines

WARSAW PACT
*Soviet forces stationed in Central Europe\**
• Total strength: 0.56 million (0.38 million in GDR)
• Tanks: about 10,000 (7,000 in Czech. and GDR)
• Fighter planes: about 2,000 (900 in GDR)
• Mediterranean Squadron (Black Sea Fleet)
• Baltic Fleet

*East European forces (Warsaw Pact)*
• Total strength: 0.85 million
• Tanks: about 14,500
• Fighter planes: about 2,250
• About 10 major surface vessels, 6 submarines

*Because of their proximity to Europe, it is necessary to add the Soviet forces stationed in the western part of the USSR and in the Caucasus region: 69 divisions (63 armored divisions).

**Deployment of American
and Allied Forces in Western Europe**

*Map supplied by General P. Gallois.*

# Chronology: Major Weapons Systems

| Year | 1945 | 1950 | 1955 | 1960 | 1965 | 1970 | 1975 | 1980 | 1983 |
|---|---|---|---|---|---|---|---|---|---|
| **Politico-military events** | | Israel 48<br>Korea 50<br>NATO 49 52 | End Vietnam I 54<br>Bandung 55<br>Hungary 56<br>Suez 56 | Kennedy 60<br>Cuba 62<br>Start Vietnam II 61 | France leaves NATO 66<br>Czech. 68<br>Six-Day War 67 | Bangladesh 71<br>Paris Accords 73<br>Yom Kippur War 73 | Fall of Saigon 75<br>Ogaden 77 | Afghanistan 79-80<br>Vietnam China 79<br>Poland 80-81 | Falklands 82<br>Lebanon 82 |
| **Nuclear events** | Hiroshima Nagasaki 45<br>Atomic bomb USSR 49 | Atomic bomb GB 52<br>H bomb US 52<br>H bomb USSR 53 | H bomb GB 57 | Atomic bomb Fr 60<br>Atomic bomb China 64 | H bomb Fr 68<br>H bomb China 67 | | Atomic bomb India 74 | | |
| **Weapons systems and vehicles — Strategic US** | | (B 47 B 52 51 53)<br>1st nuclear sub US 54 | 1st satellite Explorer 58 | Minute Man I 61<br>1st SLBM Polaris I 61<br>Titan II 62<br>Polaris III 64 MIRV | Minute Man II 66<br>Moon landing 69<br>Minute Man III MIRV 70 | Poseidon III 71 MIRV | | Trident IV 80<br>Space shuttle 81 | ACLM 82 |
| **Tactical US** | | Honest John 53 | Thor Jupiter 59-63 | Sergeant 62<br>Pershing I 64 | FB III 69<br>Lance 72 | | | | Pershing II 83<br>GLCM 83 |
| **Strategic USSR** | | | 1st SLBM SSN4 55<br>Bear 56<br>Sputnik 57<br>SSN4 57-65 | 1st ICBM SS7 61<br>SSN5 H 64 | SS9-SS11 65-66<br>Yankee 67 | | SS17 (MIRV) 75<br>SS18-SS19 74 75 | | |
| **Tactical USSR** | | | TV16 (Badger) 55<br>Scud-Frog 57<br>SS4 59 | SS5 61 | | TU 22M (Backfire) 74 | SS20 77<br>SS21-SS22-SS23 78 79 80 | | |
| **Others** | | | | Buccaneer GB 62<br>Mirage IV Fr 64 | 1st SLBM Fr.-67<br>Polaris III GB-67<br>1st missile Fr 68-70 | Pluton Fr-73<br>M20 Fr-77 | | MRBM China-80<br>S3 Fr-80 | |

Source: Pierre Saint Macary, *Conflicts in the Contemporary World,* FNSP, 1982. Revised and expanded by Michel Tatu (1983).

# American Aggressiveness as Seen by the USSR

ICELAND

AZORES

BERMUDAS

BAHAMAS

GUANTANAMO

PANAMA

ASCENSION

SEYCHELLES

DIEGO GARCIA

OKINAWA

Bases, land troops, marines

Operating stations for reconnaissance, communications, navigation, radar

Air bases

Naval bases

## Major U.S. Military Bases Abroad

*Source:* "Who Endangers the Peace?" Brochure, Ministry of Defense of the USSR, 1982.

## Soviet Aggressiveness as Seen by the United States

*Source:* C. W. Weinberger, *Soviet Military Power,* Dept. of Defense, Washington, DC, 1982.

# Distances

**km**

| | Berlin | Bombay | Buenos Aires | Cairo | Calcutta | Caracas | Copenhagen | Chicago | Darwin | Hong Kong | Honolulu | Johannesburg | Lagos | London | Los Angeles | Lisbon | Mexico | Moscow | Nairobi | New York | Paris | Peking | Reykjavik | Rio de Janeiro | Rome | Singapore | Sydney | Tokyo |
|---|---|---|---|---|---|---|---|---|---|---|---|---|---|---|---|---|---|---|---|---|---|---|---|---|---|---|---|---|
| Berlin | | | | | | | | | | | | | | | | | | | | | | | | | | | | |
| Bombay | 6288 | | | | | | | | | | | | | | | | | | | | | | | | | | | |
| Buenos Aires | 11909 | 14925 | | | | | | | | | | | | | | | | | | | | | | | | | | |
| Cairo | 2890 | 4355 | 11814 | | | | | | | | | | | | | | | | | | | | | | | | | |
| Calcutta | 7033 | 1664 | 16524 | 5699 | | | | | | | | | | | | | | | | | | | | | | | | |
| Caracas | 8435 | 14522 | 5096 | 10203 | 15464 | | | | | | | | | | | | | | | | | | | | | | | |
| Copenhagen | 357 | 6422 | 12067 | 3206 | 7072 | 8392 | | | | | | | | | | | | | | | | | | | | | | |
| Chicago | 7084 | 12953 | 9011 | 9860 | 12839 | 4027 | 6840 | | | | | | | | | | | | | | | | | | | | | |
| Darwin | 12946 | 7257 | 14693 | 11612 | 6047 | 18059 | 12903 | 15065 | | | | | | | | | | | | | | | | | | | | |
| Hong Kong | 8754 | 4317 | 18478 | 8150 | 2659 | 16360 | 8671 | 12526 | 4271 | | | | | | | | | | | | | | | | | | | |
| Honolulu | 11764 | 12914 | 12164 | 14223 | 11343 | 9670 | 11407 | 6836 | 8640 | 8921 | | | | | | | | | | | | | | | | | | |
| Johannesburg | 8870 | 6974 | 8088 | 6267 | 8459 | 11019 | 9225 | 13984 | 10639 | 10732 | 19206 | | | | | | | | | | | | | | | | | |
| Lagos | 5198 | 7612 | 7916 | 3915 | 9216 | 7741 | 5530 | 9612 | 14222 | 11854 | 16308 | 4505 | | | | | | | | | | | | | | | | |
| London | 928 | 7190 | 11131 | 3508 | 7961 | 7507 | 952 | 6356 | 13848 | 9623 | 11632 | 9071 | 5017 | | | | | | | | | | | | | | | |
| Los Angeles | 9311 | 14000 | 9852 | 12200 | 13120 | 5812 | 9003 | 2804 | 12695 | 11639 | 4117 | 16676 | 12414 | 8758 | | | | | | | | | | | | | | |
| Lisbon | 2311 | 8018 | 9600 | 3794 | 9075 | 6509 | 2478 | 6424 | 15114 | 11028 | 12587 | 8191 | 3799 | 1588 | 9122 | | | | | | | | | | | | | |
| Mexico | 9732 | 15656 | 7389 | 12372 | 15280 | 3586 | 9514 | 2726 | 14631 | 14122 | 6085 | 14585 | 11071 | 8936 | 2493 | 8676 | | | | | | | | | | | | |
| Moscow | 1610 | 5031 | 13477 | 2902 | 5534 | 9938 | 1561 | 8000 | 11350 | 7144 | 11323 | 9161 | 6254 | 2498 | 9769 | 3906 | 10724 | | | | | | | | | | | |
| Nairobi | 6370 | 4532 | 10402 | 3536 | 6179 | 11544 | 6706 | 12883 | 10415 | 8776 | 17282 | 2927 | 3807 | 6819 | 15544 | 6461 | 14818 | 6244 | | | | | | | | | | |
| New York | 6385 | 12541 | 8526 | 9020 | 12747 | 3430 | 6188 | 1145 | 16047 | 12950 | 7980 | 12841 | 8477 | 5572 | 3936 | 5422 | 3364 | 7510 | 11842 | | | | | | | | | |
| Paris | 876 | 7010 | 11051 | 3210 | 7858 | 7625 | 1026 | 6650 | 13812 | 9630 | 11968 | 8732 | 4714 | 342 | 9085 | 1454 | 9200 | 2486 | 6485 | 5836 | | | | | | | | |
| Peking | 7822 | 4757 | 19268 | 7544 | 3269 | 14399 | 7202 | 10603 | 6011 | 1963 | 8160 | 11710 | 11457 | 8138 | 10060 | 9668 | 12460 | 5794 | 9216 | 10988 | 8217 | | | | | | | |
| Reykjavik | 2385 | 8335 | 11437 | 5266 | 8687 | 6915 | 2103 | 4757 | 13892 | 9681 | 9787 | 10938 | 6718 | 1887 | 6936 | 2848 | 7460 | 3304 | 8683 | 4206 | 2228 | 7882 | | | | | | |
| Rio de Janeiro | 10025 | 13409 | 1953 | 9896 | 15073 | 4546 | 10211 | 8547 | 16011 | 17704 | 13342 | 7113 | 6035 | 9299 | 10155 | 7734 | 7693 | 11562 | 8928 | 7777 | 9187 | 17338 | 9874 | | | | | |
| Rome | 1180 | 6175 | 11151 | 2133 | 7219 | 8363 | 1531 | 7739 | 13265 | 9284 | 12916 | 7743 | 4039 | 1431 | 10188 | 1861 | 10243 | 2376 | 5391 | 6888 | 1105 | 8126 | 3297 | 9214 | | | | |
| Singapore | 9944 | 3914 | 15879 | 8267 | 2897 | 18359 | 9969 | 15078 | 3349 | 2599 | 10816 | 8660 | 11145 | 10852 | 14123 | 11886 | 16610 | 8428 | 7460 | 15339 | 10737 | 4478 | 11514 | 15712 | 10025 | | | |
| Sydney | 16096 | 10160 | 11800 | 14418 | 9138 | 15343 | 16042 | 14875 | 3150 | 7374 | 8168 | 11040 | 15519 | 16992 | 12073 | 18178 | 12696 | 14497 | 12153 | 15989 | 16962 | 8949 | 16617 | 13501 | 16324 | 6300 | | |
| Tokyo | 8924 | 6742 | 18362 | 9671 | 5141 | 14164 | 8696 | 10137 | 5431 | 2874 | 6202 | 13547 | 13480 | 9562 | 8811 | 11149 | 11304 | 7485 | 11260 | 10849 | 9718 | 2099 | 8802 | 18589 | 9861 | 5321 | 7823 | |
| Vancouver | 7980 | 12267 | 11294 | 10838 | 11445 | 6701 | 7646 | 2851 | 12215 | 10246 | 4357 | 16452 | 11951 | 7582 | 1736 | 8287 | 3945 | 8203 | 14531 | 3903 | 7923 | 8516 | 5698 | 11238 | 8991 | 12829 | 12501 | 7554 |

# World Statistical Survey

| | Land area (thousands of sq. km.) | Population, 1980 (in millions) | Density (pop./sq. km.) | Estimation of population, 2000 (in millions) | Urban population, 1980 (% total) | Life expectancy (in years) | % Adult literacy | Annual consumption of energy per person (in kilograms equiv. coal) | Contribution in calories per day & per person (1977) | GNP 1980 per person (in dollars) |
|---|---|---|---|---|---|---|---|---|---|---|
| | 1 | 2 | 3 | 4 | 5 | 6 | 7 | 8 | 9 | 10 |
| **NORTH AMERICA** | | | | | | | | | | |
| Canada | 9976 | 24 | 2 | 28 | 80 | 74 | 99 | 13200 | 3374 | 10310 |
| United States | 9363 | 228 | 24 | 259 | 77 | 73 | 99 | 11700 | 3576 | 11360 |
| **EUROPE** | | | | | | | | | | |
| Albania | 29 | 2.7 | 93 | 4 | 37 | 70 | | 1100 | 2730 | (840) |
| E. Germany | 108 | 17 | 155 | 17 | 76 | 73 | 99 | 7130 | 3641 | 7180 |
| W. Germany | 249 | 61 | 248 | 62 | 85 | 72 | 99 | 6260 | 3381 | 13590 |
| Austria | 84 | 7.5 | 90 | 8 | 54 | 72 | 99 | 5100 | 3535 | 10230 |
| Belgium | 31 | 9.8 | 321 | 10 | 72 | 73 | 99 | 6500 | 3583 | 12180 |
| Bulgaria | 111 | 9 | 81 | 10 | 64 | 73 | 98 | 5500 | 3611 | 4150 |
| Cyprus | 9 | 0.66 | 67 | | (43) | 73 | 89 | (1966) | | 3560 |
| Denmark | 43 | 5.1 | 119 | 5 | 84 | 75 | 99 | 5700 | 3418 | 12950 |
| Eire | 70 | 3.3 | 46 | 4 | 58 | 73 | 98 | 3700 | 3541 | 4880 |
| Spain | 505 | 37.5 | 74 | 43 | 74 | 73 | | 2700 | 3149 | 5400 |
| Finland | 337 | 4.9 | 14 | 5 | 62 | 73 | 100 | 6000 | 3100 | 9720 |
| France | 548 | 54 | 98 | 58 | 78 | 74 | 99 | 4800 | 3434 | 11730 |
| Greece | 132 | 9.6 | 72 | 11 | 62 | 74 | | 2160 | 3400 | 4380 |
| Hungary | 93 | 10.8 | 115 | 11 | 54 | 71 | 99 | 3800 | 3521 | 4180 |
| Iceland | 103 | 0.23 | 2 | | (88) | 76 | 99 | | | 11330 |
| Italy | 301 | 57 | 189 | 61 | 69 | 73 | 98 | 3300 | 3428 | 6480 |
| Luxembourg | 3 | 0.36 | 138 | | (68) | 72 | 99 | (14700) | (3410) | 14510 |
| Malta | 0.3 | 0.36 | 1070 | | | 72 | | (1080) | | 3470 |
| Norway | 324 | 4.1 | 13 | 4 | 53 | 75 | 99 | 11750 | 3175 | 12650 |
| Netherlands | 41 | 14.1 | 343 | 16 | 76 | 75 | 99 | 6600 | 3338 | 11470 |
| Poland | 313 | 35.8 | 115 | 42 | 57 | 71 | 98 | 5750 | 3656 | 3900 |
| Portugal | 92 | 9.9 | 106 | 11 | 31 | 71 | 72 | 1450 | 3076 | 2370 |
| Romania | 238 | 22.2 | 92 | 25 | 50 | 71 | 98 | 4660 | 3444 | 2340 |

219

| | 1 | 2 | 3 | 4 | 5 | 6 | 7 | 8 | 9 | 10 |
|---|---|---|---|---|---|---|---|---|---|---|
| United Kingdom | 245 | 56 | 229 | 58 | 91 | 73 | 99 | 5280 | 3336 | 7920 |
| Sweden | 450 | 8.3 | 18 | 8 | 87 | 75 | 99 | 8260 | 3221 | 13520 |
| Switzerland | 41 | 6.5 | 153 | 7 | 58 | 75 | 99 | 5000 | 3485 | 16440 |
| Czechoslovakia | 128 | 15.3 | 118 | 17 | 63 | 71 | 99 | 6660 | 3430 | 5820 |
| USSR | 22400 | 265 | 12 | 312 | 62 | 70 | | 5800 | 3460 | 4550 |
| Yugoslavia | 256 | 22.4 | 87 | 26 | 42 | 69 | 85 | 2420 | 3445 | 2620 |
| **ASIA** | | | | | | | | | | |
| Afghanistan | 648 | 15.9 | 24 | 24 | 15 | 37 | 12 | 88 | 2695 | (170) |
| Saudi Arabia | 2150 | 9 | 4 | 15 | 67 | 54 | 16 | 2000 | 2624 | 11260 |
| Bahrain | 0.6 | 0.4 | 620 | | (80) | 67 | (40) | (10000) | | 5560 |
| Bangladesh | 144 | 90 | 625 | 141 | 11 | 46 | 26 | 40 | 2100 | 130 |
| Burma | 677 | 35 | 48 | 54 | 27 | 54 | 70 | 67 | 2286 | 170 |
| Bhutan | 47 | 1.3 | 27 | 2 | 4 | 44 | | | 2028 | 80 |
| China | 9597 | 980 | 98 | 1245 | 13 | 64 | 66 | 734 | 2441 | 290 |
| North Korea | 121 | 18.3 | 151 | 28 | 60 | 65 | | 2775 | 2837 | (1130) |
| South Korea | 98 | 38.8 | 393 | 52 | 55 | 65 | 93 | 1473 | 2785 | 1520 |
| U. A. Emirates | 84 | 1 | 11 | 1 | 72 | 63 | 56 | 4450 | | 26850 |
| Hong Kong | 1 | 5.1 | 4900 | 6 | 90 | 74 | 90 | 1480 | 2883 | 4240 |
| India | 3288 | 680 | 207 | 994 | 22 | 52 | 36 | 194 | 2021 | 240 |
| Indonesia | 1919 | 148 | 77 | 216 | 20 | 53 | 62 | 225 | 2272 | 430 |
| Iraq | 435 | 13.1 | 30 | 23 | 72 | 56 | | 664 | 2134 | 3020 |
| Iran | 1648 | 38.8 | 23 | 61 | 50 | 59 | 50 | 1141 | 3138 | |
| Israel | 21 | 3.9 | 178 | 5 | 89 | 72 | | 3510 | 3141 | 4500 |
| Japan | 372 | 117 | 314 | 130 | 78 | 76 | 99 | 4050 | 2949 | 9890 |
| Jordan | 98 | 3.2 | 31 | 6 | 56 | 61 | 70 | 522 | 2107 | 1420 |
| Cambodia | 181 | 6.9 | 38 | 10 | (15) | | | 2 | 1926 | |
| Kuwait | 18 | 1.36 | 73 | 2 | 88 | 70 | 60 | 6160 | | 19830 |
| Laos | 237 | 3.4 | 14 | 5 | 14 | 43 | 41 | 98 | 2082 | |
| Lebanon | 10 | 2.7 | 270 | 4 | 76 | 66 | | 1028 | 2495 | |
| Malaysia | 330 | 14 | 42 | 21 | 29 | 64 | | 713 | 2610 | 1620 |
| Maldive Is. | 0.3 | 0.15 | 473 | | | 47 | 82 | | | 260 |
| Mongolia | 1565 | 1.7 | 1 | 3 | 51 | 64 | | 1483 | 2523 | (780) |
| Nepal | 141 | 14.6 | 96 | 22 | 5 | 44 | 19 | 13 | 2002 | 140 |
| Oman | 300 | 0.9 | 4 | | | 48 | | (2006) | | 4380 |
| Pakistan | 804 | 83 | 103 | 134 | 28 | 50 | 24 | 210 | 2280 | 300 |
| Philippines | 300 | 49 | 163 | 77 | 36 | 64 | 75 | 330 | 2189 | 690 |
| Qatar | 11 | 0.2 | 18 | | | 58 | | | | 26080 |
| Singapore | 0.5 | 2.4 | 4137 | 3 | 100 | 72 | | 5780 | 3074 | 4430 |

| | 1 | 2 | 3 | 4 | 5 | 6 | 7 | 8 | 9 | 10 |
|---|---|---|---|---|---|---|---|---|---|---|
| Sri Lanka | 66 | 15 | 220 | 21 | 27 | 66 | 85 | 135 | 2126 | 270 |
| Syria | 185 | 9 | 44 | 16 | 50 | 65 | 58 | 925 | 2684 | 1340 |
| Taiwan | 36 | 18 | 500 | 25 | 46 | | | | | |
| Thailand | 514 | 47 | 91 | 68 | 14 | 63 | 84 | 353 | 1929 | 670 |
| Turkey | 781 | 45 | 56 | 67 | 47 | 62 | 60 | 770 | 2907 | 1470 |
| Vietnam | 330 | 55 | 17 | 88 | 19 | 63 | 87 | 138 | 1801 | ? |
| Yemen | 195 | 7 | 35 | 11 | 10 | 42 | 21 | 58 | 2192 | 430 |
| S. Yemen | 333 | 2 | 6 | 3 | 37 | 45 | 40 | 510 | 1945 | 420 |
| | | | | | | | | | | |
| **AFRICA** | | | | | | | | | | |
| South Africa | 1221 | 30 | 24 | 52 | 50 | 61 | | 2900 | 2831 | 2300 |
| Algeria | 2382 | 19 | 8 | 34 | 44 | 56 | 35 | 645 | 2372 | 1870 |
| Angola | 1247 | 7.1 | 5 | 12 | 21 | 42 | | 200 | 2133 | 470 |
| Benin | 113 | 3.4 | 30 | 6 | 14 | 47 | 25 | 65 | 2249 | 310 |
| Botswana | 600 | 0.8 | 1 | 1.3 | (12) | 50 | (35) | | | 910 |
| Burundi | 28 | 4.1 | 153 | 7 | 2 | 42 | 23 | 17 | 2254 | 200 |
| Cameroon | 475 | 8.4 | 17 | 14 | 35 | 47 | | 143 | 2069 | 670 |
| Cape Verde Is. | 4 | 0.32 | 78 | | (20) | 61 | | (143) | | 300 |
| Central African Rep. | 623 | 2.3 | 3 | 4 | 41 | 44 | 39 | 46 | 2242 | 300 |
| Comoros Is. | 2 | 0.34 | 147 | | | (50) | | (52) | | 300 |
| Congo | 342 | 1.6 | 4 | 3 | 45 | 59 | | 195 | 2284 | 900 |
| Ivory Coast | 322 | 8.4 | 25 | 15 | 40 | 47 | 41 | 230 | 2517 | 1150 |
| Djibouti | 22 | 0.4 | 18 | | | 45 | 14 | (823) | | 480 |
| Egypt | 1001 | 41 | 40 | 60 | 45 | 57 | 44 | 540 | 2760 | 580 |
| Ethiopia | 1222 | 31 | 24 | 54 | 14 | 40 | 15 | 20 | 1754 | 140 |
| Gabon | 268 | 0.55 | 2 | | (32) | 45 | | (1830) | | 4400 |
| Ghana | 239 | 12 | 46 | 23 | 36 | 49 | | 260 | 1983 | 420 |
| Guinea | 246 | 5.5 | 19 | 9 | 19 | 45 | 20 | 83 | 1943 | 290 |
| Guinea-Bissau | 36 | 0.57 | 15 | | | 42 | 28 | (62) | | 160 |
| Equat. Guinea | 28 | 0.36 | 12 | | | 47 | | (105) | | |
| Upper Volta | 274 | 6.1 | 24 | 10 | 10 | 39 | 5 | 26 | 1875 | 210 |
| Kenya | 583 | 16 | 26 | 36 | 14 | 55 | 50 | 172 | 2032 | 420 |
| Lesotho | 30 | 1.3 | 43 | 2 | 12 | 51 | 52 | | 2245 | 420 |
| Liberia | 111 | 1.9 | 16 | 4 | 28 | 54 | 25 | 425 | 2404 | 530 |
| Libya | 1760 | 3 | 2 | 5 | 30 | 56 | 50 | 2250 | 2985 | 8640 |
| Madagascar | 587 | 8.7 | 14 | 16 | 18 | 47 | 50 | 90 | 2486 | 350 |
| Malawi | 118 | 6.1 | 48 | 12 | 10 | 44 | 25 | 67 | 2066 | 230 |
| Mali | 1240 | 7 | 5 | 13 | 17 | 43 | 9 | 28 | 2117 | 190 |
| Morocco | 447 | 20 | 42 | 36 | 40 | 56 | 28 | 302 | 2534 | 900 |

| | 1 | 2 | 3 | 4 | 5 | 6 | 7 | 8 | 9 | 10 |
|---|---|---|---|---|---|---|---|---|---|---|
| Mauritius | 2 | 1 | 452 | (1,8) | (44) | 65 | 85 | (407) | | 1060 |
| Mauritania | 1031 | 1.5 | 1 | 3 | 23 | 43 | 17 | 196 | 1976 | 440 |
| Mozambique | 783 | 12 | 13 | 22 | 9 | 47 | 28 | 120 | 1906 | 230 |
| Namibia | 825 | 1.01 | 1 | (1,8) | | | | | | |
| Niger | 1267 | 5.3 | 4 | 10 | 13 | 43 | 5 | 46 | 2139 | 330 |
| Nigeria | 924 | 85 | 90 | 169 | 20 | 49 | 30 | 80 | 1951 | 1010 |
| Uganda | 236 | 13 | 54 | 24 | 9 | 54 | 48 | 39 | 2110 | 300 |
| Rwanda | 26 | 5.2 | 171 | 10 | 4 | 45 | 50 | 28 | 2264 | 200 |
| São Tomé & Principe | 1 | 0.1 | 103 | | | | | (173) | | 490 |
| Senegal | 197 | 5.7 | 27 | 10 | 32 | 43 | 10 | 253 | 2261 | 450 |
| Seychelles Is. | 0.3 | 0.1 | 220 | | (27) | 66 | | (583) | | 1770 |
| Sierra Leone | 72 | 3.5 | 46 | 6 | 22 | 45 | | 84 | | 280 |
| Somalia | 638 | 4 | 6 | 7 | 30 | 44 | 60 | 74 | 2150 | |
| Sudan | 2506 | 19 | 7 | 34 | 25 | 46 | 20 | 133 | 2033 | |
| Swaziland | 17 | 0.55 | 33 | 1 | (8) | 47 | 65 | | 2184 | 410 |
| Tanzania | 945 | 19 | 20 | 36 | 12 | 52 | 66 | 51 | | 680 |
| Chad | 1284 | 4.1 | 3 | 7 | 18 | 41 | 15 | 22 | 2063 | 280 |
| Togo | 57 | 2.5 | 43 | 5 | 20 | 47 | 18 | 112 | 1762 | 120 |
| Tunisia | 164 | 6.5 | 37 | 10 | 52 | 60 | 62 | 590 | 2069 | 410 |
| Zaire | 2345 | 29 | 12 | 51 | 34 | 47 | 58 | 100 | 2674 | 1310 |
| Zambia | 753 | 5.8 | 7 | 11 | 43 | 49 | 44 | 832 | 2271 | 220 |
| Zimbabwe | 391 | 7.4 | 18 | 17 | 23 | 55 | 74 | 783 | 2002 | 560 |
| | | | | | | | | | 2576 | 630 |

**LATIN AMERICA**

| | 1 | 2 | 3 | 4 | 5 | 6 | 7 | 8 | 9 | 10 |
|---|---|---|---|---|---|---|---|---|---|---|
| Argentina | 2767 | 28 | 10 | 34 | 82 | 70 | 93 | 1960 | 3347 | 2390 |
| Bahamas | 14 | 0.24 | 16 | | (58) | 69 | 93 | (7350) | | 3790 |
| Belize | 23 | 0.16 | 7 | | | | | (598) | | 1080 |
| Bolivia | 1099 | 5.6 | 5 | 9 | 33 | 50 | 63 | 447 | 1974 | 570 |
| Brazil | 8512 | 119 | 14 | 177 | 68 | 63 | 76 | 1020 | 2562 | 2050 |
| Chile | 757 | 11 | 14 | 15 | 80 | 67 | | 1153 | 2656 | 2150 |
| Colombia | 1139 | 27 | 23 | 39 | 70 | 63 | | 914 | 2364 | 1180 |
| Costa Rica | 51 | 2.2 | 41 | 3 | 43 | 70 | 90 | 812 | 2550 | 1730 |
| Cuba | 115 | 9.8 | 83 | 12 | 65 | 73 | 96 | 1360 | 2720 | (1410) |
| Dominique | 0.5 | 0.08 | 170 | | | | | (203) | | 620 |
| El Salvador | 21 | 4.5 | 206 | 8 | 41 | 63 | 62 | 338 | 2051 | 660 |
| Ecuador | 284 | 8 | 28 | 14 | 45 | 61 | 81 | 640 | 2104 | 1270 |

Source: *Report on World Development, 1982,* World Bank.
*Note:* Earlier sources or other sources in parentheses.

| | 1 | 2 | 3 | 4 | 5 | 6 | 7 | 8 | 9 | 10 |
|---|---|---|---|---|---|---|---|---|---|---|
| Grenada | 0.8 | 0.1 | 130 | | | 69 | | (209) | | 690 |
| Guatemala | 109 | 7.3 | 61 | 12 | 39 | 59 | | (260) | 2156 | 1080 |
| Guyana | 215 | 0.9 | 4 | 1.5 | (46) | 70 | | (1070) | | 690 |
| Haiti | 28 | 5 | 174 | 7 | 28 | 53 | 23 | 63 | 2100 | 270 |
| Honduras | 112 | 3.7 | 31 | 7 | 36 | 58 | 60 | 238 | 2015 | 560 |
| Jamaica | 11 | 2.2 | 195 | 3 | 41 | 71 | 90 | 1326 | 2660 | 1040 |
| Barbados | 0.4 | 0.25 | 620 | | (46) | 71 | 99 | (1100) | | 3040 |
| Mexico | 1973 | 70 | 36 | 115 | 67 | 65 | 81 | 1535 | 2654 | 2090 |
| Nicaragua | 130 | 2.6 | 18 | 5 | 53 | 56 | 90 | 446 | 2446 | 740 |
| Panama | 77 | 1.8 | 25 | 3 | 54 | 70 | | 895 | 2341 | 1730 |
| Paraguay | 407 | 3.2 | 7 | 5 | 39 | 65 | 84 | 234 | 2824 | 1300 |
| Peru | 1285 | 18 | 13 | 27 | 67 | 58 | 80 | 716 | 2274 | 930 |
| Dominican Rep. | 49 | 5.5 | 112 | 6 | 51 | 61 | 67 | 156 | 2094 | 1160 |
| St. Lucia | 0.7 | 0.12 | 195 | | | | | (392) | | 900 |
| St. Vincent | 0.4 | 0.12 | 300 | | | | | (211) | | 520 |
| Surinam | 163 | 0.4 | 2 | | | 89 | 65 | (2150) | | 2840 |
| Trinidad & Tobago | 5 | 1.2 | 240 | 2 | (23) | 72 | 95 | 4870 | 2694 | 4370 |
| Uruguay | 176 | 2.9 | 16 | 4 | 84 | 71 | 94 | 1220 | 3036 | 2810 |
| Venezuela | 912 | 15 | 14 | 24 | 83 | 67 | 82 | 2950 | 2435 | 3630 |
| **AUSTRALIA AND THE PACIFIC** | | | | | | | | | | |
| Australia | 7687 | 14.5 | 2 | 17 | 89 | 74 | 100 | 6540 | 3428 | 9820 |
| New Zealand | 269 | 3.3 | 12 | 4 | 85 | 73 | 66 | 4700 | 3345 | 7090 |
| Papua-New Guinea | 462 | 3 | 9 | 5 | 18 | 51 | 32 | 300 | 2268 | 780 |
| Fiji | 18 | 0.63 | 33 | | (37) | 75 | 65 | (466) | | 1850 |
| Kiribati | 1 | 0.07 | 71 | | (30) | | | (317) | | |
| Nauru | 0.02 | 0.008 | 380 | | | | | (7000) | | |
| Solomon | 28 | 0.22 | 8 | | (10) | | | (200) | | 480 |
| Western Samoa | 3 | 0.16 | 56 | | (21) | | 68 | (187) | | |
| Tonga | 0.7 | 0.1 | 142 | | | | | (169) | | |
| Tuvalu | | | | | | | | | | |
| Vanuatu (New Hebrides) | 15 | 0.11 | 7 | | (24) | | | (480) | | 530 |

# Bibliographical References

*Report on World Development.* World Bank. Washington, DC, annual.

Ramsès. *Annual Report of the French Institute of International Relations.* Paris, annual.

*World Economic Outlook.* International Monetary Fund. Washington, DC, annual.

*Economic Perspectives.* OECD. Paris, annual.

*Strategic Survey.* International Institute for Strategic Studies. London, annual.

*The Military Balance.* International Institute for Strategic Studies. London, annual.

*SIPRI Yearbook.* Stockholm.

Specialized publications of the Documentation française. Paris.

Specialized publications of the U.S. Department of State. Washington, DC.

Among the French journals: *Politique internationale, Commentaire, Défense nationale, Stratégique, Études polémologiques, Géopolitique, Hérodote* (the only journal of geography that integrates the geopolitical dimension).

Among the English-language journals: *Foreign Affairs, Foreign Policy, The Washington Quarterly.*